The Disease Prevention Cookbook

Clara Schneider
MS, RD, RN, LD, CDE

SMALL STEPS PRESS

Publisher, John Fedor; *Managing Editor, Books,* Abe Ogden; *Associate Director, Consumer Books,* Sherrye Landrum; *Editor,* Gregory L. Guthrie; *Composition,* Circle Graphics, Inc.; *Cover Design,* Koncept, Inc.; *Printer,* Worzalla

Printed in the United States of America
1 3 5 7 9 10 8 6 4 2

Small Steps Press is an imprint of the American Diabetes Association. For information about Small Steps Press or the American Diabetes Association, in English or Spanish, call 1-800-342-2383. To order other Small Steps books, call 1-800-232-6733.

Consult a health care professional before trying any of the suggestions in this publication. Small Steps Press and ADA assume no responsibility for any injury that may result from the suggestions or information in this publication.

⊗ The paper in this publication meets the requirements of the ANSI Standard Z39.48-1992 (permanence of paper).

Small Steps Press titles may be purchased for business or promotional use or for special sales. To purchase this book in large quantities, or for custom editions of this book with your logo, contact Lee Romano Sequeira, Special Sales & Promotions, at the address below, or at Lees@smallstepspress.com or 703-299-2046.

Small Steps Press
1701 North Beauregard Street
Alexandria, Virginia 22311

Library of Congress Cataloging-in-Publication Data

Schneider, Clara G.
  Disease prevention cookbook / Clara Schneider.
      p. cm.
  Includes bibliographical references and index.
  ISBN 1-58040-195-3 (alk. paper)
  1. Diabetes—Diet therapy—Recipes. 2. Medicine, Preventive. I. Title.

  RC662.S363 2005
  641.5'6314—dc22
                                              2005009551

Dedication

In memory of Eleanor.

Contents

Acknowledgments

First and foremost, I owe gracious thanks to my family for all of their support in helping make this book happen. My husband Philip provided unwavering moral support and helped with the shopping, cooking, recipe testing, and editing. My daughter Amy is my best lay editor. With a stake in preventing diabetes, heart disease, cancer, and stroke for her father, brother, and self, she was especially good at identifying sections for revision so that nonmedical people can understand this book. My son Stephen also helped with testing and selecting recipes.

My sister Elizabeth Frasco lent an ear to problems and offered suggestions as they came along. I also wish to thank my mother and father, Constance and Edward Garbus, for their support. Rick Pellegrini generously offered the use of his cooking skills. Thanks, Rick, for your apples direct from your tree. Thanks to Richard O'Donnell for his stories and music. Classical music is a wonderful accompaniment to cooking and writing.

The dietitians at Inova HealthSource in Fairfax, Virginia (Susan Baum, RD; Christine Spengler, RD; and Diane Silvester, RD), kindly proofread and provided technical suggestions for this book.

Every single one of the food councils used in this book was wonderfully supportive. They are very knowledgeable in the foods that they promote. If you have questions about a food, do not hesitate to contact the associated council. In each recipe, you will find the websites for these councils.

I am especially grateful to my father-in-law Philip. He presents an outstanding example of a person who has lived with diabetes for over 30 years. It is remarkable to see a 91-year-old man ride his bicycle or go swimming at least three times a week, even though he says he is the slowest person in the pool. It is wonderful to see a person take control of his health rather than allowing it to control him.

Introduction

You've probably heard about them—the increasing dangers of developing diabetes, stroke, heart disease, and cancer for the average American. Our growing sedentary lifestyle and oversized food portions put many people at risk of developing this quartet of diseases, but while many have heard of the risks, few people truly understand what these risks are and how they relate to the diseases that threaten many of us.

This is primarily a cookbook, but you will also find that it serves as a guide to making you aware of what and how much you eat. This is possibly one of the most important health-conscious decisions you can make, because although people know that there is an increased risk of diabetes, stroke, cancer, and heart disease in our society, they don't know that many of the risk factors—anything that raises your chances of developing a disease—can be staved off by simple lifestyle decisions: reaching and maintaining a healthy body weight, exercising moderately, and eating a nutritious diet. It doesn't take a scientist to see that these three decisions are closely interrelated. Just browsing the recipes in this book will show that by controlling how much you eat and the nutrients in your food, you can begin making progress on maintaining your body weight, creating a healthy diet, and lowering your risk for disease.

Hopefully, this book will also set straight the myth that eating healthy has to include tasteless entrees or involve mysterious ingredients that aren't on your local supermarket's shelves. Just about all of these healthy recipes come from our nation's food councils, experts in creating delightful dishes from everyday favorite foods. They were wonderful to work with in building this book, and I encourage you to seek even more recipes off their websites, which are included on almost every page.

Before we jump directly to the food, though, we should consider what these diseases are and how they affect you. I will also try to dispel as many popular disease myths as possible.

What Is Diabetes?

Diabetes is a chronic, but manageable, disease that affects the way a body uses glucose. Your body turns the food you consume into glucose, which is then ushered into your cells by insulin to be converted into energy. When you have diabetes, your body doesn't make enough insulin or doesn't use the insulin it does make very well, causing glucose to build up in the bloodstream. All of that unused glucose in your blood begins to negatively affect most of your body's systems. Although not normally identified as a cause of death, many of this disease's complications (the other diseases that arise from having diabetes, such as kidney failure, stroke, and heart disease) result in life-threatening conditions.

Diabetes is diagnosed through measuring your blood sugar levels. When the levels of glucose in your blood are over 200 mg/dl, or 126 mg/dl if you have not been eating, you are diagnosed with diabetes. You may have also heard of the term "pre-diabetes." Pre-diabetes indicates that a person has high blood glucose levels (110–125 mg/dl), but not high enough to be diagnosed with diabetes, and is at greater risk of developing full-blown diabetes in the future. It is during this stage that you can make lifestyle changes to avoid developing diabetes and live a longer, healthier life. Scientific studies in people with pre-diabetes have shown that certain lifestyle changes, such as reducing your body weight by 7% (if you are obese) and exercising for 150 minutes per week, can help reduce the risk of developing diabetes by 58%.

If diabetes is not properly managed, its complications can include reduced vision or vision loss, kidney failure, ulcers in the legs and feet (sometimes resulting in amputation), gum disease, and increased occurrence of strokes and heart attacks.

Types of Diabetes

There are several different kinds of diabetes, but these three main classifications are most common.

Type 1 diabetes. This type of diabetes is an autoimmune disease, which means that for reasons still unknown the body attacks and destroys itself. In type 1 diabetes (once called insulin-dependent diabetes or juvenile diabetes), the body's immune system destroys specific cells in the pancreas, called beta cells. Beta cells make the hormone insulin, which helps glucose (sugar) get into our cells. Without beta cells, your body cannot produce insulin, which is why all people with type 1 diabetes have to take insulin. You can use these recipes if you have type 1 diabetes, but they will not help prevent type 1. If you have type 1 diabetes, see a registered dietitian, who will design a meal plan specifically for you.

Type 2 diabetes. Type 2 diabetes is a disease in which the body doesn't make enough insulin for its needs or the body doesn't use insulin well (called insulin resistance). Because increased insulin resistance is often associated with obesity, weight loss and a healthy diet are the best way to prevent the development of type 2 diabetes.

Gestational diabetes. Gestational diabetes mellitus (GDM) is diagnosed in 4% of pregnant women. Being pregnant releases hormones in the body that increase the need for insulin. Women with GDM cannot make enough insulin during pregnancy to keep their blood sugar in the normal range. After the pregnancy, GDM can evolve into type 2 diabetes or it can simply resolve itself as blood glucose levels return to normal values. Women who have GDM need to follow a special diet and sometimes require insulin during pregnancy. Doctors carefully watch women with GDM because high sugar levels can harm the unborn baby. After the pregnancy is over, women who have had GDM should follow a healthy lifestyle, keep a healthy weight, exercise, and maintain a healthy diet to avoid developing type 2 diabetes.

Risk Factors for Diabetes

How and why people develop diabetes is still being studied, but a person's genetic background plays a major role. If members of your family have diabetes, then you run a much greater risk of developing the disease yourself. Although there is no known prevention for type 1 diabetes, it has been shown that diet and exercise are effective in preventing type 2 diabetes, the most common type of diabetes. In addition to family history, there are a number of other diabetes risk factors, and they include

- ethnicity: African Americans, Native Americans, Latinos, Asian Americans, and Pacific Islanders
- obesity and inactive lifestyles
- high blood pressure (at or above 130/80 mmHg)
- high LDL cholesterol (the "bad" cholesterol) and high triglycerides
- women who had a baby that weighed more than nine pounds at birth or who had GDM during pregnancy

What Are Stroke and Heart Disease?

Stroke

Contrary to what many people believe, a stroke does not affect the heart, but instead the brain cells. When someone has a stroke, an artery carrying blood to the brain clogs or ruptures, preventing the brain from getting oxygen. Because a stroke affects the blood vessel system, it is a type of cardiovascular disease even though it does not have a direct effect on the heart. A stroke is a very serious condition, but many of its risk factors are preventable.

According to the American Stroke Association, someone in America has a stroke every 45 seconds and one person dies of a stroke every 3 minutes. Survivors can be partially paralyzed, have difficulty with speech, be unable to understand others, exhibit depressive symptoms, and become dependent on others for help with the activities of daily living.

Types of Strokes

There are four different types of stroke.

Thrombotic stroke (cerebral thrombosis). When a thrombus (clot) forms in an artery in or leading to the brain, a thrombotic stroke occurs. Individuals with high cholesterol and clogged or hardened arteries (atherosclerosis) are at risk for these. Atherosclerosis is a long process, beginning in childhood, with plaque deposits building up over many years. When the artery becomes blocked, the affected part of the brain no longer receives oxygen or nutrients and dies quickly. This type of stoke usually occurs at night or in the early part of the morning and is frequently seen in elderly people. A thrombotic stroke often follows a transient ischemic attack.

Transient ischemic attack (TIA). TIA is usually considered an advanced warning sign of a bigger stroke to come. With the formation of a clot, a person will have symptoms such as affected speech or paralysis of a limb, but this effect normally passes. TIAs affect the body for a few hours or up to 24 hours.

Cerebral embolism. A traveling clot, also called an embolism, causes a cerebral embolism. A cerebral embolism occurs when an embolism forms in another part of the body, travels through the bloodstream, and becomes stuck in an artery of the brain.

Stroke due to hemorrhage. When an artery ruptures in the brain and releases a lot of blood (a hemorrhage), a stroke due to hemorrhage occurs. The bleeding causes pressure, swelling the brain so much that it does not receive oxygen and nutrition. This type of stoke can be caused by high blood pressure or an aneurysm (a weak spot in an artery that causes a ballooning of the artery wall). If the aneurysm breaks, it will cause a hemorrhage. Sometimes symptoms will slowly go away over time.

Heart Disease

The term heart disease (sometimes called cardiovascular disease or CVD) covers all conditions that affect the heart. Generally, heart disease develops over time and is the leading cause of death in the United States. Coronary heart disease (CHD) is a type of heart disease that healthy weight, exercise, and low-saturated-fat diet can help prevent. CHD is very much like a thrombotic stroke, except that the clogged artery is in or leads to the heart rather than the brain. If the heart does not have enough oxygen, a person may experience angina (chest or heart pain). Another condition, called silent ischemia (or silent heart attack), occurs when the heart does not get enough oxygen but the patient has no pain. If the clot completely blocks off the blood supply, a "heart attack" occurs and portions of the heart will die. Very often, the patient dies. According to data from the American Heart Association, in 2002, one in every five deaths in the United States was due to a heart attack.

Risk Factors for Stroke and Heart Disease

Because atherosclerosis begins very early in childhood, it is good to know the risk factors and make family lifestyle changes for yourself and your children right away. Children as young as 2 years old can usually follow the same disease prevention diet as adults. Consult your child's pediatrician or dietitian about an adequate diet for healthy growth. Control the following risks to decrease the likelihood of stroke and heart attack:

- Smoking: do not smoke and avoid secondhand smoke. If you take oral contraceptives and you smoke, your risks increase dramatically.
- Elevated blood pressure: there is an increased risk at 115/75 mmHg and it doubles with each increase of 20/10 mmHg. Normal blood pressure is under 120/80 mmHg. If your blood pressure is between 120/80 and 139/89 mmHg, you have pre-hypertension, and if it is over 140/90, you have hypertension (high blood pressure).
- High blood cholesterol: the target range for cholesterol is below 200 mg/dl for total cholesterol. An HDL cholesterol (sometimes called "good" cholesterol) level above 60 mg/dl helps reduce the risk of heart disease and stroke. A safe LDL cholesterol (or "bad" cholesterol) level is less than 100 mg/dl, and normal triglyceride (the storage form of fat in the body) levels should be less than 150 mg/dl.
- Lack of exercise (sedentary lifestyle): this is what is being referred to when you hear doctors talking about sedentary lifestyle. Exercise is important for keeping your body healthy. Everyone should have some exercise in his or her daily lifestyle. Be sure to consult your doctor before beginning any exercise regimen.
- Obesity: if you are overweight or obese, ask your doctor about a weight-loss program. You can also use one of the meal plans in this book.
- Diabetes: this disease is a serious contributor to stroke and heart disease. If you have diabetes, take care to keep your blood sugar, blood pressure, and cholesterol levels in the target ranges.

What Is Cancer?

In 2004, cancer was the most common cause of death in people less than 85 years of age. Cancer is a disease in which cells begin to grow out of control and then produce more and more abnormal cells that spread throughout the body. It can begin anywhere in the body and is classified based on where the abnormal growth starts. This means that if kidney cancer spreads to the heart, the cancer in the heart still behaves like kidney cancer. Doctors call this spread of cancerous (or malignant) cells "metastasis." There are many risk factors for the development of cancer, including viruses, radiation, certain chemicals, tobacco, the food we eat, and a lack of certain nutrients. The American Institute for Cancer Research estimates that diet, lack of exercise, and obesity are risk factors linked to at least 30% of all cancers.

To decrease your risk for cancer, try to maintain a healthy weight, exercise, and eat a variety of whole grains, fruits, and vegetables. Many fruits and vegetables have phytochemicals, which are plant chemicals that may decrease your cancer risk. To reduce the risk of cancer, doctors recommend that you control the amount of fat and sodium in your diet. When you do have fats, eat foods with monounsaturated fats rather than other, less healthy foods with saturated fat or *trans*-fats (such as fatty meats, palm and coconut oil, and whole milk). Foods that are high in monounsaturated fat include most nuts, avocado, and canola and olive oil.

Risk Factors for Cancer

There are many risk factors for cancer and, like with most diseases, not all of them are easily controlled. Your genetic background is determined by birth and not by lifestyle choice. But you can make lifestyle decisions that will have a positive impact on your health. The following list identifies some preventable risk factors for cancer.

- Smoking
- Being overweight or obese
- Lack of exercise
- Diet
- Alcohol (recent studies have indicated that there is a link between alcohol and breast cancer in women)
- Proper skin care (for example, avoiding sunburn)

Ask your doctor for appropriate age- and sex-related screening tests for cancer. These include tests for colon, prostate, and female cancers. Many cancers are treatable and curable if detected early.

Disease Myths

Due to the human body's complicated systems, it can be difficult to understand how diseases develop and operate in your body. Myths and misunderstandings about diseases arise out of this lack of knowledge. You can't prevent or treat a disease if you don't have the correct information about it, and sometimes believing a disease myth can actually cause you to do things that increase your risk or make a condition worse. Here are some common myths about diseases that should be demystified.

Myth 1: Nothing Can Be Done to Prevent Diabetes, Heart Disease, Stoke, or Cancer

These diseases share many common risk factors. You can help prevent all of them by exercising, keeping a healthy weight, and not smoking. Limiting the saturated fats, *trans*-fats, and cholesterol in your diet will help. Try to follow a nutritious diet that includes monounsaturated fats instead of other less healthy fats. Exercise as often as you can.

Myth 2: Diabetes Skips a Generation

When I was writing this book and discussing the topic with friends, a few of them did not believe that they were at risk for diabetes. They all had a parent with diabetes and believed that diabetes skips a generation. *Diabetes does not skip a generation; a family history of the disease is a very clear risk factor.* Every generation needs to take care of themselves to help prevent diabetes. You are actually at increased, not lowered, risk of developing diabetes if your parent or parents have the disease.

Myth 3: Eating Sugar Causes Diabetes

Some people believe that a diet that contains sugar causes diabetes. *A diet that contains sugar is not a risk factor for diabetes.* Remember, it is the body's inability to process glucose properly that defines diabetes, not eating it.

Myth 4: Only Adults Need to Worry about Preventing Diabetes, Stroke, Heart Disease, and Cancer

In the past decade, a startling number of obese children and adolescents have developed type 2 diabetes. This is a disturbing trend because type 2 diabetes normally develops only in fully grown adults. Blood pressure and atherosclerosis problems may begin in childhood, leading to early stroke and heart disease. There is a lot of research on this, and many experts think that overeating and little exercise are the source of the problem. Good eating habits should start in early childhood, which will lead to healthy routines through adulthood. A low-saturated-fat diet that includes fruits, vegetables, and whole-grain foods is a healthy start.

Calculating Your Disease Risk

If your doctor thinks that you may be at risk of developing one of these diseases, he or she may look at your body mass index, commonly called BMI. Your BMI is a calculation based on your height and weight that helps evaluate whether you are at a healthy weight. An increase in BMI is usually associated with an increase in body fat and an increased risk of diabetes, heart disease, stroke, and cancer. However, BMI values may not be correct for all people; the chart isn't as accurate for those who are overly tall or short and it doesn't take into consideration the amount of muscle (which is more dense than fat; therefore, a handful of muscle weighs more than a handful of fat) a person has. Typically, however, BMI is a very accurate measurement of someone's weight and disease risk. Use Table 1 to determine your BMI.

Once you have found your BMI, it is time to determine your disease risk. The National Heart, Lung, and Blood Institute suggests that cross-referencing your

TABLE 1. Body Mass Index Table

To use the table, find your height in the left-hand column labeled Height. Move across to your weight. The number at the top of the column is the BMI at that height and weight. Pounds have been rounded off.

BMI	19	20	21	22	23	24	25	26	27	28	29	30	31	32	33	34	35
Height (inches)								**Body Weight (pounds)**									
58	91	96	100	105	110	115	119	124	129	134	138	143	148	153	158	162	167
59	94	99	104	109	114	119	124	128	133	138	143	148	153	158	163	168	173
60	97	102	107	112	118	123	128	133	138	143	148	153	158	163	168	174	179
61	100	106	111	116	122	127	132	137	143	148	153	158	164	169	174	180	185
62	104	109	115	120	126	131	136	142	147	153	158	164	169	175	180	186	191
63	107	113	118	124	130	135	141	146	152	158	163	169	175	180	186	191	197
64	110	116	122	128	134	140	145	151	157	163	169	174	180	186	192	197	204
65	114	120	126	132	138	144	150	156	162	168	174	180	186	192	198	204	210
66	118	124	130	136	142	148	155	161	167	173	179	186	192	198	204	210	216
67	121	127	134	140	146	153	159	166	172	178	185	191	198	204	211	217	223
68	125	131	138	144	151	158	164	171	177	184	190	197	203	210	216	223	230
69	128	135	142	149	155	162	169	176	182	189	196	203	209	216	223	230	236
70	132	139	146	153	160	167	174	181	188	195	202	209	216	222	229	236	243
71	136	143	150	157	165	172	179	186	193	200	208	215	222	229	236	243	250
72	140	147	154	162	169	177	184	191	199	206	213	221	228	235	242	250	258
73	144	151	159	166	174	182	189	197	204	212	219	227	235	242	250	257	265
74	148	155	163	171	179	186	194	202	210	218	225	233	241	249	256	264	272
75	152	160	168	176	184	192	200	208	216	224	232	240	248	256	264	272	279
76	156	164	172	180	189	197	205	213	221	230	238	246	254	263	271	279	287

To use the table, find your height in the left-hand column labeled Height. Move across to your weight. The number at the top of the column is the BMI at that height and weight. Pounds have been rounded off.

Body Weight (pounds)

BMI → Height (inches) ↓	36	37	38	39	40	41	42	43	44	45	46	47	48	49	50	51	52	53	54
58	172	177	181	186	191	196	201	205	210	215	220	224	229	234	239	244	248	253	258
59	178	183	188	193	198	203	208	212	217	222	227	232	237	242	247	252	257	262	267
60	184	189	194	199	204	209	215	220	225	230	235	240	245	250	255	261	266	271	276
61	190	195	201	206	211	217	222	227	232	238	243	248	254	259	264	269	275	280	285
62	196	202	207	213	218	224	229	235	240	246	251	256	262	267	273	278	284	289	295
63	203	208	214	220	225	231	237	242	248	254	259	265	270	278	282	287	293	299	304
64	209	215	221	227	232	238	244	250	256	262	267	273	279	285	291	296	302	308	314
65	216	222	228	234	240	246	252	258	264	270	276	282	288	294	300	306	312	318	324
66	223	229	235	241	247	253	260	266	272	278	284	291	297	303	309	315	322	328	334
67	230	236	242	249	255	261	268	274	280	287	293	299	306	312	319	325	331	338	344
68	236	243	249	256	262	269	276	282	289	295	302	308	315	322	328	335	341	348	354
69	243	250	257	263	270	277	284	291	297	304	311	318	324	331	338	345	351	358	365
70	250	257	264	271	278	285	292	299	306	313	320	327	334	341	348	355	362	369	376
71	257	265	272	279	286	293	301	308	315	322	329	338	343	351	358	365	372	379	386
72	265	272	279	287	294	302	309	316	324	331	338	346	353	361	368	375	383	390	397
73	272	280	288	295	302	310	318	325	333	340	348	355	363	371	378	386	393	401	408
74	280	287	295	303	311	319	326	334	342	350	358	365	373	381	389	396	404	412	420
75	287	295	303	311	319	327	335	343	351	359	367	375	383	391	399	407	415	423	431
76	295	304	312	320	328	336	344	353	361	369	377	385	394	402	410	418	426	435	443

Adapted from the National Heart, Lung, and Blood Institute (www.nhlbi.nih.gov/guidelines/obesity/bmi_tbl.htm).

BMI and waist circumference is one of the better ways to assess your risk for type 2 diabetes, hypertension, and heart disease. To find your risk level, refer to Table 2.

If you have found that you are at an increased risk of developing a disease and are overweight, weight loss may be a great way to help prevent this from happening. Recent scientific studies in diabetes have shown that if an at-risk person loses 7% of his or her body weight, he or she has a 58% less chance of developing diabetes. For example, if you weigh 180 pounds, you will want to lose 13 pounds ($180 \times 0.07 = 12.6$). If Table 2 shows that you are at risk, ask your doctor if it would be healthy for you to lose 7% of your weight. Then, ask him or her if one of the food plans presented in this book will help you head toward a healthier lifestyle. Be sure that your doctor knows about any special dietary needs you may have.

Getting Healthy and Preventing Disease

Weight-Loss Programs

There are many ways to lose weight in a healthy manner. It is often helpful to attend exercise programs, support groups, and classes. Many success stories in weight loss depend on personal preferences. Some of us like to learn in groups, and some people work better on their own.

No matter how you approach it, a very important factor in weight loss is your diet. If your doctor approves, you may want to try one of the meal plans

TABLE 2. Risk of Developing a Disease

To determine your disease risk, find your BMI (which you determined in Table 1) in the left-hand column and then read to the right until you are in the column that matches your waist size. Inside that box, you will find your risk of developing diabetes, cancer, and/or heart disease.

	Waist circumference	
BMI (kg/m²)	**Men** (40 inches or less) **Women** (35 inches or less)	**Men** (more than 40 inches) **Women** (more than 35 inches)
18.5	Normal	Normal
18.5–24.9	Normal	Normal (sometimes Increased)
25.0–29.9	Increased	High
30.0–34.9	High	Very high
35.0–39.9	Very high	Very high
40 or more	Extremely high	Extremely high

Adapted from the National Heart, Lung, and Blood Institute (www.nhlbi.nih.gov).

included in this book and, if you have success after a month, keep going with it. However, it is always best to discuss meal plans and dieting with a nutrition professional. These people are called registered dietitians (RDs), and they can help you develop a healthy diet and good eating habits. If you want to find an RD in your area, here are good places to start:

1. Ask your doctor for a recommendation.
2. Call your local hospital to see if they have outpatient services. Ask to talk to the clinical dietitian.
3. Call the American Dietetic Association at 1–800–366–1655 and ask for a list of RDs in your area. You can also get information from their website: www.eatright.org.

Lifestyle Changes

Before you can make healthy changes to your lifestyle, you need to evaluate what your current lifestyle is. Your lifestyle is a wide variety of activities, habits, and behaviors that make up your daily living. It includes the amount of exercise you get, what you eat and when, how much sleep you get, and so on. Not all changes to your lifestyle are dramatic, though, so don't think that seeing an RD or doctor is going to turn you into a morning person after you've been a night owl your entire life. Baby steps are the key to disease risk reduction.

Still, to prevent disease, you'll have to make permanent changes. Don't think of your diet as temporary, but as a change to how you eat from now on. For the first step, you'll be asked to write down everything you eat in a small book or chart for 4–7 days in order to study what you are currently eating. Follow the sample chart below.

Food	Time	With whom did you eat?	Where were you?	Were you hungry?	What were you doing?

Write down absolutely everything. If you see a candy bowl and have a piece, write it down. If you have a soda, write it down. Anything you eat, write it down. Many people are shocked to find out just how much they really eat in a day.

Become familiar with the time of day that you usually eat. Carefully evaluate what kind of eater you are. Are you eating unnecessary calories between supper and bedtime? Where were you when you ate? Some people eat more than they should when they eat out. Some people eat because it is mealtime and not because they are hungry. Do you do this? The last column is very important because what you do while eating can influence your eating habits. Some people eat more when they are in front of the television or they have different habits on the weekend. You should consider all of the lifestyle factors that contribute to your eating habits.

The key to making lifestyle changes is recognizing and changing patterns. For example, do you find that you are not even aware of eating at certain times? Perhaps you go to the fridge during every commercial break and don't even notice. That is a pattern. If you don't write down that snack, you might not know you ate anything. Ask your family for help in identifying patterns and in giving support and encouragement. Be confident that you can make these changes yourself and stick with them.

Focus on Good Nutrition

In this book are the tools you need to establish a balanced, nutritious, lifelong eating plan. Most nutritionists agree that a balanced diet contains a wide variety of fruits, vegetables, whole grains, beans, low-fat dairy products, and protein foods. These foods also contain fiber, which is necessary for a healthy diet. Most people should have around 20–35 g of fiber a day. Eating a wide variety of foods gives you the nutrients and fiber your body needs.

Get control of how much fat is in your diet. Eating large quantities of saturated fat, cholesterol, and *trans*-fat increases your risk for diseases. *Trans*-fats are found in some baked goods, margarines, and shortening and are used to increase shelf life. *Trans*-fat plus saturated fat should only provide less than 10% of your daily calories. Beginning in January 2006, the federal government will require all food manufacturers to provide *trans*-fat information on their nutrition labels. This is important for you because it'll allow you to determine the kind of fat you eat and what items on the supermarket shelves to avoid. Generally, experts consider monounsaturated fat the healthiest in our diet. Current research shows that this fat does not increase your risk for cancer or increase LDL cholesterol levels, which lead to heart disease and stroke. Most nuts, canola oil, and olive oil are high in monounsaturated fat. Still, everyone needs some fat in their diet to absorb fat-soluble vitamins, to provide essential fatty acids, and to feel satisfied after a meal.

Current thinking is that it is beneficial to have foods high in omega-3 fatty acids in your diet as long as a health professional decides that it is healthy for you (some people are allergic to such foods or may have other diseases that may make eating them unsafe). Some scientists have found that eating omega-3 fatty acids helps decrease the risk of some cancers, decreases artery clogging, decreases the risk of irregular heartbeats, and helps prevent excessive blood clotting. Foods that contain omega-3 fatty acids include canola oil, olive oil, walnuts, flax seed, soybeans, salmon, tuna, herring, lake trout, scallops, halibut, and green leafy vegetables. The American Diabetes Association recommends having two to three servings of fish a week. However, before you increase the amount of fish you eat, you should talk with a doctor. Certain chemicals in some fish can affect children and pregnant women (or women trying to conceive). If you have a family history of female cancer or have had female cancer, ask your doctor if you should avoid soy and flax products, too. Pregnant and nursing women, infants, and children should consult a doctor before using flax products.

Ask your physician and RD to help you plan what is right for you.

Diet Choices and Weight Loss

After counseling many people in nutrition over the years, I have found that with exercise, most women can lose weight and then stay in a healthy range on a diet of 1500–1800 calories per day. Most men need 1800–2000 calories per day to lose weight and then maintain that weight. It is important for you to decide how to use your meal plan.

To start using this book and reduce disease risk requires you to take two more steps. First, select which calorie plan will work best for you from the table below. Remember that it is still important to eat enough calories to stay healthy and fuel yourself for exercise. Women usually need 1500–1800 calories a day, and men need 1800–2000 calories a day. The table below indicates the number of exchanges you will have with the calorie plan you select. If you consume the

Exchange Lists			
	1500 calories	**1800 calories**	**2000 calories**
Starch	7	7	8
Fruit	3	4	5
Milk (fat-free)	2	3	3
Vegetables (nonstarchy)	4	4	5
Lean Meats	5	6	6
Fats	5	7	8

Note: These values are rounded. If you were to add up the calories for these exchanges, the actual totals are 1520 calories for the 1500 calorie diet, 1815 calories for the 1800 calorie diet, and 2025 calories for the 2000 calorie diet.

corresponding amounts of calories, the values in the boxes indicate the number of exchanges you can eat for each category.

Next, read the following examples of weight-loss plans. There are four, each with their own specific systems. People are unique and different plans are successful for each individual, so choose the plan that appeals to you most.

Plan 1: Meal plans with food divided into breakfast, lunch, dinner, and snacks. This plan uses the Exchange Lists for Weight Management (co-published by the American Diabetes Association and the American Dietetic Association). This meal-planning tool groups similar foods into lists of items that have approximately the same amounts of different nutrients (such as carbohydrate, protein, and fat). You can then choose a program in which a certain number of exchange values are given for each meal and trade your food servings between different lists, which is why they are called exchanges. For a full list of exchanges, you can purchase a copy of the Exchange Lists for Meal Planning (item no. 5601-04) or Exchange Lists for Weight Management (item no. 5603-04) through the American Diabetes Association by calling 1-800-232-6733 or visiting their website at http://store.diabetes.org.

Exchange lists intimidate many people, and you may have heard they are complicated. However, they really aren't that difficult to understand, especially when you have a guidebook containing exchange values or when your cook-book tells you how many exchange values are contained in a recipe, like in this book. For example, breakfast for a 1500 calorie diet includes 2 starch exchanges, 1 fruit, 1 fat-free milk, 1 lean meat, and 1 fat. For this plan, you could have two slices of whole-wheat bread (starch), a small orange (fruit), 1 cup of nonfat milk (fat-free milk), 1/4 cup of 4.5%-fat cottage cheese (lean meat), and 1/2 Tbsp peanut butter (fat) for your bread. Now, if you wanted more starch in another meal, you can simply remove one of the slices of bread from the meal above and have an extra starch exchange for the rest of the day. So, if you really want an extra 1/2 cup of mashed potatoes (1 starch exchange) for dinner, you've saved space in your meal plan for them.

If you want a plan that is spelled out to the letter, Plan 1 is the choice for you. See sample plans on pages 15 and 16.

> **TIP**
>
> Measure all of your foods. Extra servings and calories come from guessing amounts.

> **TIP**
>
> If you do not eat at least three servings of dairy or calcium-fortified foods every day, ask your doctor if you should take a calcium supplement. People who include low-fat dairy products in their diet have a lower risk of osteoporosis. If you cannot tolerate calcium products and want to use these meal plans, you can substitute a starch or fruit exchange for each milk exchange.

1500 Calorie Plan

Breakfast	2 starch	1 fruit	1 milk (nonfat)	1 lean meat	1 fat
Lunch	2 starch	1 fruit	1 vegetable*	2 lean meat	1 fat
Midafternoon snack	1 starch	1 vegetable*	1 fat		
Dinner	2 starch	1 fruit	1 milk	2 vegetable*	2 lean meat
					2 fat

*Vegetables are from the nonstarchy vegetable exchange list.
Note: Use no more than 12–17 g of saturated fat plus *trans*-fat a day.

1800 Calorie Plan

Breakfast	2 starch	1 milk (nonfat)	1 fruit	1 lean meat	2 fat
Lunch	2 starch	1 fruit	1 vegetable*	2 lean meat	2 fat
Midafternoon snack	1 starch	1 fruit	1 vegetable*	1 fat	

Continued

1800 Calorie Plan (Continued)

Dinner	2 starch	1 milk (nonfat)	2 vegetable*	1 fruit	3 lean meat	2 fat
Snack	1 milk (nonfat)					

*Vegetables are from the nonstarchy vegetable exchange list.

Note: Use no more than 14–20 g of saturated plus *trans*-fat a day.

2000 Calorie Plan

Breakfast	2 starch	1 milk (nonfat)	1 fruit	1 lean meat	2 fat
Lunch	2 starch	2 fruit	2 vegetable*	2 lean meat	2 fat
Midafternoon snack	1 starch	1 fruit	1 vegetable*	1 fat	
Dinner	2 starch	1 milk (nonfat)	2 vegetable*	1 fruit	3 lean meat	2 fat
Snack	1 milk (nonfat)	1 starch	1 fat		

*Vegetables are from the nonstarchy vegetable exchange list.

Note: Use no more than 16–22 g of saturated fat plus *trans*-fat a day.

Plan 2: Checking off foods as you eat them. Instead of counting exchanges for every meal, you can count the exchanges for the day. With this approach, you have a set number of starch, fruit, milk, meat, and fat exchanges per day. You will check off items on a list as you eat during the day.

Your plan could look like this if you have prearranged food amounts but decide when to eat them. Check off the boxes as you eat them and make sure that you eat at least three times during the day.

1500 Calorie Plan							
Starch (7 exchanges)							
Fruit (3 exchanges)							
Nonfat milk (2 exchanges)							
Vegetables (4 exchanges)							
Lean meat and meat substitutes (5 exchanges)							
Fats (4 exchanges)							

Note: Use no more than 12–17 g of saturated fat plus *trans*-fat per day.

1800 Calorie Plan							
Starch (7 exchanges)							
Fruit (4 exchanges)							
Nonfat milk (3 exchanges)							
Vegetables (4 exchanges)							
Lean meat and meat substitutes (6 exchanges)							
Fats (7 exchanges)							

Note: Use no more than 14–20 g of saturated fat plus *trans*-fat per day.

Continued

2000 Calorie Plan									
Starch (8 exchanges)									
Fruit (5 exchanges)									
Nonfat milk (3 exchanges)									
Vegetables (5 exchanges)									
Lean meats and meat substitutes (6 exchanges)									
Fats (8 exchanges)									

Note: Use no more than 16–22 g of saturated fat plus *trans*-fat a day.

Plan 3: Counting carbohydrates and fats. You can count and eat a set amount of carbohydrates and fats per day. For this plan, you will need to carefully read food labels and use cookbooks that have grams of total fat and saturated fat per serving listed in the recipe. Try to consume no more than a total of 12–17 g of saturated fat and *trans*-fats in the 1500 calorie diet, 14–20 g of saturated fat and *trans*-fats in the 1800 calorie diet, and 16–22 g of saturated fat and *trans*-fats in the 2000 calorie diet. These amounts add up to 7–10% of the calories you eat. You will need to incorporate 5–6 oz of protein per day into your diet.

If you follow a 1500 calorie diet, with 55% of calories from carbohydrates and 30% of calories from fat, your total daily carbohydrate intake should be 206 g, your total daily fat intake should be 50 g per day, and of this amount, you should have no more than 12–17 g of saturated fat and *trans*-fat. You should have 5 oz of lean protein per day.

If you follow an 1800 calorie diet, with 49% of calories from carbohydrates and 30% of calories from fat, your total daily carbohydrate intake should be 221 g, your total daily fat intake should be 60 g, of which no more than 14–20 g should be saturated fat and *trans*-fat. You should have 6 oz of lean protein per day.

If you follow a 2000 calorie diet, with 51% of calories from carbohydrates and 30% of calories from fat, your total daily carbohydrate intake should be 256 g, your total daily fat intake should be 66 g, with no more than 16–22 g of saturated fat and *trans*-fat. You should have 6 oz of lean protein per day.

Plan 4: Counting carbohydrate choices. When some people count carbohydrates, they count carbohydrate choices. A carbohydrate choice equals 15 grams of carbohydrate. You can find many carbohydrate choices in the exchange list books by the American Diabetes Association. If you do this, a 1500 calorie diet would have 13–14 carbohydrate choices. Fruit, milk, and starch exchanges have approximately 15 grams of carbohydrate in them. Each fruit, milk, or starch exchange equals one carbohydrate choice. If you have a wide assortment of nonstarchy vegetables in your day, you may want to decrease the carbohydrate choices to 12 because 1/2 cup of nonstarchy vegetables has about 5 grams of carbohydrate.

When you count carbohydrate choices, you will be checking off boxes as you eat 1 carbohydrate choice.

1500 Calorie Plan												
Carbohydrate (12 choices)												

Note: Count your fat grams (50 total), including no more than 12–17 g of saturated fat plus *trans*-fat. Eat many nonstarchy vegetables. Eat 5 oz of protein.

1800 Calorie Plan														
Carbohydrate (14 choices)														

Note: Count your fat grams (60 total), including no more than 14–20 g of saturated fat plus *trans*-fat. Eat many nonstarchy vegetables. Eat 6 oz of protein.

2000 Calorie Plan															
Carbohydrate (16 choices)															

Note: Count your fat grams (66 total), including no more than 16–22 g of saturated fat plus *trans*-fat. Eat many nonstarchy vegetables. Eat 6 oz of protein.

Keeping Track

Before you begin any weight-loss program, you need to know from where you're starting. This is a great way to motivate yourself further and find out if your plan is working in an appealing way. Here is a short to-do list:

- with a tape measure, measure your abdomen circumference at the navel
- with a tape measure, measure the circumference of your thighs 12–14 inches up from the middle of your kneecap
- with a tape measure, measure your arm circumference 6–9 inches down from the top of your shoulder
- record this information with the date in a logbook

Repeat these measurements once a week. Pick a regular time every week to do this and review your progress. Many people make the mistake of watching the scale too closely when they begin to diet. This is counterproductive because losing weight takes time, and some people become discouraged when they do not see immediate results. Remember to keep a positive attitude toward your new diet and lifestyle changes.

Also, while you get fit, you may sometimes find that your weight does not dramatically change. This is because muscle is more dense than fat. This is good. You are building muscle and losing fat. You will still be losing inches off your body, which will reduce your disease risk.

Exercise

The two most important disease prevention tools are probably the simplest. Diet and exercise are the keys to a healthy, long life. Everyone should get some exercise, and recent studies have shown that exercising for at least 150 minutes a week (only 30 minutes for 5 days a week) will radically reduce your risk of developing a disease. Still, for some people who have not exercised recently, a sudden increase in exercise can be dangerous, so always discuss starting and developing an exercise plan with your doctor.

The easiest way to start exercising is to make walking one of your daily activities. It can be fun walking around your neighborhood with family and friends, and it is a great first step in developing a healthy lifestyle. Talk to your doctor about starting a walking program and using a pedometer, a small, inexpensive device that clips onto your belt and measures the number of steps you take. You can get one at your local drugstore, on the Internet, or through the American Diabetes Association. For healthy individuals, experts recommend taking 10,000 steps per day. Start by measuring the number of steps you take on a normal day. Try adding 100–200 steps a day until you reach 10,000 or more. Wear the pedometer while you exercise. If you like to dance, play tennis, bowl, or do any activity that involves taking steps or walking, you can count all these toward your total steps for the day. If you like activities that do not involve taking steps, such as rowing or swimming, set aside a certain amount of time to exercise. Hold firm to the schedule you make and just do it. Wearing a pedometer works; personal experience has shown me that. As a registered dietitian who was eating correctly, I realized that I needed to exercise to lose weight. I lost 12 pounds by increasing to 10,000 steps per day.

You may also want to join a fitness center or take exercise classes through a community program. Exercise buddies work, too. Ask a friend to exercise with you, and you'll find that you can motivate each other to succeed. A good friend of mine jogs every day. He has a friend who wanted to run a charity mini-marathon but had never run before for more than 10 minutes at a time. Her goal was to run 5 kilometers (3.1 miles) in 30 minutes. They decided to train together every day for 4 weeks. Every day, they increased the distance and pace of their run. On the last day of her training, she was able to meet her goal. She ran the mini-marathon and finished the race. She had the help and encouragement of a friend who wanted her to succeed. When people exercise together, they do not want to disappoint each other. Plus, they both lost 8 pounds and still run together. Now, think about someone who will be a good exercise buddy for you.

Keep Drinking Water

Remember to drink water before, during, and after exercise. Ask your doctor how much you should drink. To figure out how much fluid a normal healthy adult needs to drink, use the following equation:

Divide your weight in pounds by 17.6, which gives you the cups of fluid you need per day.

Here is an example, say you weigh 150 pounds. Thus, you will figure out your weight like this:

$$150 \text{ pounds} \div 17.6 = 8.5 \text{ cups of water a day}$$

Double check with your doctor to make sure this is acceptable for you. You may need more than this if you exercise strenuously or less if you have certain health problems.

You need to exercise. I can't emphasize this enough. Tell yourself to find something you like and do it; it's that easy. Record everything, too, just like what you eat. Take down what type of exercise you do and how long you exercise if you are working out during a specific time. If you are using a pedometer, record your daily steps and set goals that steadily increase. Remember, exercise can and should be fun. Think of it as an opportunity to pursue an activity that you haven't had the time for in the past.

Bringing It Together

I wrote this book to help you move toward a healthier, disease-free lifestyle. It may look like an ordinary cookbook, but it is actually much, much more. By combining exercise and diet, you will bring yourself closer to a longer, healthier life and avoid many of the common risks for disease that affect most people.

The recipes in this book are very tasty and include all of the information you need to follow a healthy diet. A variety of the food councils in North America provided them. I believe that, because of their expertise on their individual foods, they have some of the best-tasting recipes. Look through the recipes and plan your food for at least 3 days to 1 week ahead of time. Remember to ask your doctor if the meal plans in this book will work for you.

What are you waiting for? Soon you'll see that living a healthy lifestyle is not only fun and active, but also filled with great meals.

Breakfast

100% Whole-Wheat Bread (Bread Machine)

Serving Size: 1 slice, **Total Servings:** 8 slices (1-lb loaf)

1 cup water (80°F)
1 Tbsp nonfat dry milk
1 Tbsp butter or margarine
1 Tbsp honey
1 tsp salt
2 1/4 cups whole-wheat flour
1 Tbsp wheat gluten
1 1/4 tsp active dry yeast

1. Bring all ingredients to room temperature. Measure ingredients accurately; for the flour, stir it, spoon into a dry measuring cup, and level off.

2. Place the ingredients in the pan in the order specified in the bread machine's instruction manual. Select the whole-wheat/wheat cycle and medium crust. If the machine does not have a whole-wheat cycle, compensate by using the basic white cycle, letting the machine operate through the first kneading cycle, then restarting it.

3. Check the consistency of the dough after 5 minutes into the kneading cycle. It should be in a moist soft ball. If the dough is too dry, add 1 Tbsp of liquid at a time. If it is too wet, add 1 Tbsp of flour at a time.

4. If the machine does not have a cooling cycle, remove the bread from the pan and cool on a wire rack. The machine's delay timer may be used.

Variants

1 1/2-lb loaf (12 slices)

1 1/2 cups water (80°F)
1 1/2 Tbsp nonfat dry milk
1 1/2 Tbsp butter or margarine
1 1/2 Tbsp honey
1 1/2 tsp salt
3 1/4 cups whole-wheat flour
1 1/2 Tbsp wheat gluten
1 1/2 tsp active dry yeast

2-lb loaf (16 slices)

1 3/4 cup water (80°F)
2 Tbsp nonfat dry milk
2 Tbsp butter or margarine
2 Tbsp honey
1 3/4 tsp salt
4 1/4 cups whole-wheat flour
2 Tbsp wheat gluten
2 1/4 tsp (1 pkg) active dry yeast

EXCHANGES*
2 Starch

Calories	146
Calories from Fat	19
Total Fat	2 g
Saturated Fat	1.0 g
Polyunsaturated Fat	0.3 g
Monounsaturated Fat	0.5 g
Cholesterol	4 mg
Sodium	311 mg
Total Carbohydrate	27 g
Dietary Fiber	4 g
Sugars	3 g
Protein	6 g

*Nutritional information is for the 1-lb loaf only.

FITTING YOUR PLAN

CALORIE PLAN	
1500	1 serving 100% Whole-Wheat Bread, 1 small apple, 8 oz nonfat milk, 1 oz low-fat ham or 1 oz cheese with less than 3 g of fat, and 1 Tbsp low-fat margarine.
1800	1 serving 100% Whole-Wheat Bread, 1 small apple, 8 oz nonfat milk, 1 oz low-fat ham or 1 oz cheese with less than 3 g of fat, and 2 Tbsp low-fat margarine.
2000	1 serving 100% Whole-Wheat Bread, 1 small apple, 8 oz nonfat milk, 1 oz low-fat ham or 1 oz cheese with less than 3 g of fat, and 2 Tbsp low-fat margarine.

This recipe courtesy of the Kansas Wheat Commission (www.kswheat.com).

Banana Orange Muffins

Serving Size: 1 muffin, **Total Servings:** 12

1/2 cup orange juice
   1 Tbsp grated orange peel
   2 Tbsp canola oil
   2 large eggs
   1 cup mashed ripe bananas (about
    2 medium)
1/4 cup honey
1/4 cup firmly packed brown sugar
   2 cups quick-cooking oatmeal
   1 cup whole-wheat flour
   2 tsp baking powder
1/2 tsp salt
1/2 cup chopped walnuts

1. Preheat oven to 400°F.

2. Combine first six ingredients in a large mixing bowl; stir well. In a medium bowl, combine brown sugar, oats, flour, baking powder, salt, and nuts. Combine with liquid ingredients and mix slightly until dry ingredients are moistened.

3. Spray muffin cups with nonstick spray and fill 3/4 full. Bake for 20 minutes or until golden brown.

EXCHANGES

2 Carbohydrate   1 1/2 Fat

Calories	212
Calories from Fat	67
Total Fat	7 g
Saturated Fat	1.0 g
Polyunsaturated Fat	3.6 g
Monounsaturated Fat	2.4 g
Cholesterol	36 mg
Sodium	171 mg
Total Carbohydrate	33 g
Dietary Fiber	3 g
Sugars	15 g
Protein	6 g

FITTING YOUR PLAN

For the meal plan below, the carbohydrates are counted as starch exchanges.

CALORIE PLAN

1500 (borrow 1/2 fat exchange from another part of the day): 1 Banana Orange Muffin, 3/4 cup canned grapefruit sections, 8 oz nonfat milk, and 1 egg cooked with nonfat cooking spray.

1800 1 Banana Orange Muffin, 3/4 cup canned grapefruit sections, 8 oz nonfat milk, 1 egg, and 1/2 tsp margarine.

2000 1 Banana Orange Muffin, 3/4 cup canned grapefruit sections, 8 oz nonfat milk, 1 egg, and 1/2 tsp margarine.

This recipe courtesy of the Wheat Foods Council (www.wheatfoods.org).

Blueberry-Apple Frosty

Serving Size: 1 cup, **Total Servings:** 4

2 cups fresh or slightly thawed
frozen blueberries
1 cup apple juice
1 cup vanilla frozen yogurt
1/2 cup milk
3/4 tsp ground cinnamon

1. Place all ingredients in a food
processor or blender; whirl until
smooth. Serve immediately.

EXCHANGES
2 Carbohydrate

Calories	131
Calories from Fat	15
Total Fat	2 g
Saturated Fat	1.1 g
Polyunsaturated Fat	0.2 g
Monounsaturated Fat	0.4 g
Cholesterol	6 mg
Sodium	35 mg
Total Carbohydrate	28 g
Dietary Fiber	2 g
Sugars	21 g
Protein	3 g

FITTING YOUR PLAN

One way to fit this recipe into breakfast, using the 2 carbohydrate exchanges in the meal pattern, is to use 1 fruit and 1 fat-free milk exchange.

CALORIE PLAN

1500   (save 1 lean-meat exchange for another meal in the day): 1 serving Blueberry-Apple Frosty, 2 slices raisin bread (1 oz each), 1/2 Tbsp peanut butter, and 2 tsp light blueberry jam.

1800   (save 1 lean-meat exchange for another meal in the day): 1 serving Blueberry-Apple Frosty, 2 slices raisin bread (1 oz each), 1 Tbsp peanut butter, and 2 tsp light blueberry jam.

2000   (save 1 lean-meat exchange for another meal in the day): 1 serving Blueberry-Apple Frosty, 2 slices raisin bread (1 oz each), 1 Tbsp peanut butter, and 2 tsp light blueberry jam.

This recipe courtesy of U.S. Highbush Blueberry Council (www.ushbc.org).

Blueberry Lemon Scones

Serving Size: 1 scone, **Total Servings:** 12

Nonstick cooking spray
2 2/3 cups all-purpose flour
1/2 cup sugar, plus 2 Tbsp (divided)
1/2 cup dried blueberries
2 1/2 tsp baking powder
1 tsp baking soda
1/2 tsp salt
1 container (8 oz) low-fat lemon yogurt
1/3 cup Dried Plum Puree or 1 jar (2 1/2 oz) baby food plums
3 Tbsp low-saturated-fat margarine
1 Tbsp freshly grated lemon rind
2 tsp vanilla extract
1/4 tsp ground nutmeg

1. Heat oven to 400°F. Lightly coat large baking sheet with nonstick cooking spray; set aside.

2. In a large bowl, combine flour, 1/2 cup sugar, blueberries, baking powder, and salt; set aside.

3. In a small bowl, whisk together yogurt, Dried Plum Puree, margarine, lemon peel, and vanilla. Add to dry ingredients and stir together with rubber spatula to form dough that just holds together. Turn dough out onto lightly floured surface and pat it into a 10-inch circle. Combine the remaining 2 Tbsp sugar with nutmeg and sprinkle evenly over the dough. Pat the sugar mixture gently. Cut circle into 12 wedges with a sharp knife.

4. Space scones about an inch apart on prepared baking sheet; bake 15–17 minutes or until scones are a rich golden brown and cracked on tops. Transfer to cooling rack; let cool slightly. Serve warm.

Dried Plum Puree

2/3 cup (4 oz) pitted dried plums
3 Tbsp water

In a food processor, combine dried plums and water; process on and off until finely chopped. Makes 1/2 cup.

EXCHANGES

3 Starch	1/2 Fat	1 Fruit

Calories 231
    Calories from Fat 31
Total Fat . . . . 3 g
    Saturated Fat . . . . 0.7 g
    Polyunsaturated Fat. . . . . 1.0 g
    Monounsaturated Fat . . . . 1.4 g
Cholesterol . . . . 1 mg
Sodium. . . . . 320 mg
Total Carbohydrate . . . . 46 g
    Dietary Fiber. 2 g
    Sugars . . . . 20 g
Protein . . . . 4 g

FITTING YOUR PLAN

CALORIE PLAN

1500 (borrow 1 starch exchange from the midafternoon snack): 1 Blueberry Lemon Scone, 6 oz fat-free (100 calories or less) yogurt, 1 oz Canadian bacon, and 1 1/2 tsp reduced-fat margarine.

1800 (borrow 1 starch exchange from the midafternoon snack and save 1 fat exchange for later in your day): 1 Blueberry Lemon Scone, 6 oz fat-free (100 calorie or less) yogurt, 1 oz Canadian bacon, and 1 1/2 tsp reduced-fat margarine.

2000 (borrow 1 starch exchange from the midafternoon snack and save 1 fat exchange for later in your day): 1 Blueberry Lemon Scone, 6 oz fat-free (100 calories or less) yogurt, 1 oz Canadian bacon, and 1 1/2 tsp reduced-fat margarine.

This recipe courtesy of the California Dried Plum Board (www.californiadriedplums.org).

Blueberry-Filled Dutch Pancake

Serving Size: 1/3 recipe, **Total Servings:** 3

1 Tbsp canola oil
3 eggs
1/2 cup nonfat milk
1/3 cup all-purpose flour
3 Tbsp sugar, divided
1/4 tsp salt (*optional*)
1 1/2 cups fresh or frozen blueberries
(thawed and drained if frozen)
1/4 tsp ground cinnamon
1/2 cup sliced bananas

1. Preheat oven to 450°F. Place oil in a 9-inch pie plate or a 9- or 10-inch ovenproof skillet (to make handle ovenproof, wrap completely with aluminum foil); tilt plate to coat evenly with oil.

2. Meanwhile, in a medium bowl combine the eggs, milk, flour, 1 Tbsp sugar, and salt until smooth. Pour batter into plate; bake for 8 minutes. Reduce heat to 375°F; bake until pancake is golden brown and sides are puffy, about 8–10 minutes longer.

3. While that is baking, combine blueberries with the remaining 2 Tbsp sugar and the cinnamon in a small bowl.

4. Remove pancake from oven; scatter bananas over pancake. Spoon blueberries over bananas. Cut into wedges; serve immediately.

Note: For more servings, double all ingredients; bake in a 13 X 9 X 2-inch baking pan for about 20–25 minutes at 425°F.

EXCHANGES

1 Starch	1 Medium-Fat Meat
1 Fruit	1 Fat

Calories	288
Calories from Fat	90
Total Fat	10 g
Saturated Fat	2.0 g
Polyunsaturated Fat	2.2 g
Monounsaturated Fat	4.7 g
Cholesterol	212 mg
Sodium	93 mg
Total Carbohydrate	41 g
Dietary Fiber	3 g
Sugars	24 g
Protein	10 g

FITTING YOUR PLAN

Because lean meat contains 3 g of fat per ounce and medium-fat meat contains 5 g of fat per ounce, with this meal pattern, you are eating an extra 2 g of fat (approximately 1/2 fat exchange). This is taken into account in the patterns below.

CALORIE PLAN

1500 (borrow 1/2 fat exchange from another meal in the day, but add 1 starch exchange to another meal): 1 serving Blueberry-Filled Dutch Pancake and 8 oz nonfat milk.

1800 (give 1/2 fat exchange and 1 starch exchange to another meal in the day): 1 serving Blueberry-Filled Dutch Pancake and 8 oz nonfat milk.

2000 (give 1/2 fat exchange and 1 starch exchange to another meal in the day): 1 serving Blueberry-Filled Dutch Pancake and 8 oz nonfat milk.

This recipe courtesy of the U.S. Highbush Blueberry Council (www.ushbc.org).

Country Breakfast Muffins or Crumpets

Serving Size: 1 sandwich, **Total Servings:** 1

1/2 medium Bartlett pear, sliced
1 oz low-fat cooked turkey sausage
1 English muffin (both halves), toasted, or crumpet
1/2 oz reduced-fat Swiss cheese, shredded

1. Sauté fresh Bartlett pear slices with precooked crumbled sausage. Arrange on toasted English muffins or crumpets. Sprinkle with cheese; heat and serve.

EXCHANGES

1 1/2 Starch	1 Medium-Fat Meat	1 Fruit

Calories	257
Calories from Fat	44
Total Fat	5 g
Saturated Fat	1.9 g
Polyunsaturated Fat	0.8 g
Monounsaturated Fat	1 g
Cholesterol	23 mg
Sodium	570 mg
Total Carbohydrate	39 g
Dietary Fiber	4 g
Sugars	10 g
Protein	14 g

FITTING YOUR PLAN

The meal plans are based on lean meat selections, and the medium-fat meat has 2 more grams of fat than the lean meat. This is approximately equal to 1/2 fat exchange or 22 calories from fat. The fat has been subtracted for the different suggested plans.

CALORIE PLAN

1500   (save 1/2 starch and 1/2 fat exchange for another meal in the day): 1 serving Country Breakfast Muffin, 1/2 cup pears, and 8 oz nonfat milk.

1800   (save 1/2 starch and 1 1/2 fat exchange for another meal in the day): 1 serving Country Breakfast Muffin, 1/2 cup pears, and 8 oz nonfat milk.

2000   (save 1/2 starch and 1 1/2 fat exchange for another meal in the day): 1 serving Country Breakfast Muffin, 1/2 cup pears, and 8 oz nonfat milk.

This recipe courtesy of the California Pear Advisory Board (www.calpear.com).

Cracked Wheat Cereal

Serving Size: 1/2 cup, **Total Servings:** 4

1 1/2 cups water
1/8 tsp salt
3/4 cup cracked wheat

1. In a small saucepan, add water and salt and bring to a boil. Quickly stir in the cracked wheat and continue stirring to prevent lumps. Reduce heat to simmer; cover and cook for about 15 minutes. Stir occasionally.

EXCHANGES
1 1/2 Starch

Calories	113
Calories from Fat	7
Total Fat	1 g
Saturated Fat	0.2 g
Polyunsaturated Fat	0.3 g
Monounsaturated Fat	0.1 g
Cholesterol	0 mg
Sodium	76 mg
Total Carbohydrate	23 g
Dietary Fiber	4 g
Sugars	0 g
Protein	5 g

FITTING YOUR PLAN

CALORIE PLAN	
1500	(save 1/2 starch exchange for later in the day): 1 serving Cracked Wheat Cereal, 4 rings of dried apples, 8 oz nonfat milk, 2 scrambled egg whites, and 1 tsp margarine.
1800	(save 1/2 starch exchange for later in the day): 1 serving Cracked Wheat Cereal, 4 rings of dried apples, 8 oz nonfat milk, 2 scrambled egg whites, 1 tsp margarine, and 6 mixed nuts.
2000	(save 1/2 starch exchange for later in the day): 1 serving Cracked Wheat Cereal, 4 rings of dried apples, 8 oz nonfat milk, 2 scrambled egg whites, 1 tsp margarine, and 6 mixed nuts.

This recipe courtesy of the Wheat Foods Council (www.wheatfoods.org).

Dried Cherry Banana Bread

Serving Size: 1 slice, **Total Servings:** 20 servings (1 loaf)

1/2 cup low-saturated-fat margarine
3/4 cup granulated sugar
  2 eggs
  2 cups unsifted, all-purpose flour
  3 tsp baking powder
1/2 tsp salt
1/4 tsp ground nutmeg
  1 cup mashed banana (about 3 medium)
  1 cup dried tart cherries

1. Combine margarine and sugar in a large mixing bowl. Beat with an electric mixer on medium speed for 3–4 minutes or until well mixed.

2. Add the eggs one at a time, beating well after each addition.

3. Combine flour, baking powder, salt, and nutmeg. Add this flour mixture and the bananas to the margarine mixture, alternating between them, and beat just until the ingredients are moistened. Do not overmix. Fold in dried cherries.

4. Pour batter into a greased 9 X 5 X 3-inch loaf pan. Bake in a preheated 350°F oven for 50–60 minutes or until done.

5. Let cool in the pan on a wire rack for 5 minutes, then remove from pan. Let cool completely. Cover in plastic wrap to store. This bread is best served the day after baking.

EXCHANGES

1 1/2 Carbohydrate	1 Fat

Calories 153	
Calories from Fat 47	
Total Fat . . . . 5 g	
Saturated Fat . . . . 1.1 g	
Polyunsaturated Fat. . . . . 1.5 g	
Monounsaturated Fat . . . . 2.3 g	
Cholesterol. . . . . 21 mg	
Sodium. . . . . 167 mg	
Total Carbohydrate . . . . 25 g	
Dietary Fiber. 1 g	
Sugars . . . . 13 g	
Protein . . . . 2 g	

FITTING YOUR PLAN

The carbohydrates in the exchanges are considered 1/2 starch and 1 fruit.

CALORIE PLAN

1500	1 serving Dried Cherry Banana Bread, 3/4 cup grits, 8 oz nonfat milk, 1 egg cooked with non-fat cooking spray, and 2 tsp light jam.
1800	(save 1 fat exchange for another meal in the day): 1 serving Dried Cherry Banana Bread, 3/4 cup grits, 8 oz nonfat milk, 1 egg cooked with nonfat cooking spray, and 2 tsp light jam.
2000	(save 1 fat exchange for another meal in the day): 1 serving Dried Cherry Banana Bread, 3/4 cup grits, 8 oz nonfat milk, 1 egg cooked with nonfat cooking spray, and 2 tsp light jam.

This recipe courtesy of the Cherry Marketing Institute (www.usacherries.com).

French Apple Yogurt

Serving Size: 1 cup, **Total Servings:** 4

3 cups diced or sliced apples
1/2 cup water
2 cups low-fat plain yogurt
1 tsp vanilla
1/2 tsp cinnamon
2 tsp brown sugar (*optional,* if apples are tart★)

★The optional brown sugar has not been included in the nutritional analysis.

1. Cook the apples in the water for 5–10 minutes or until soft.

2. Reserve 1 cup and put the rest into blender with 1 cup yogurt, vanilla, cinnamon, and brown sugar. Blend very briefly.

3. Mix all ingredients together.

EXCHANGES

1/2 Fruit	1 Fat-Free Milk

Calories 126	
Calories from Fat 18	
Total Fat . . . . 2 g	
Saturated Fat . . . . 1.1 g	
Polyunsaturated Fat. . . . . 0.1 g	
Monounsaturated Fat . . . . 0.5 g	
Cholesterol . . . . 7 mg	
Sodium. . . . . 102 mg	
Total Carbohydrate . . . . 22 g	
Dietary Fiber. . . . . 2 g	
Sugars . . . . 15 g	
Protein . . . . 7 g	

FITTING YOUR PLAN

CALORIE PLAN	
1500	1 serving French Apple Yogurt, 1/2 small apple, 2-oz bagel, 1 1/2 Tbsp reduced-fat cream cheese, and 1 poached egg.
1800	1 serving French Apple Yogurt, 1/2 small apple, 2-oz bagel, 1 1/2 Tbsp reduced-fat cream cheese, 1 tsp margarine, and 1 poached egg.
2000	1 serving French Apple Yogurt, 1/2 small apple, 2-oz bagel, 1 1/2 Tbsp reduced-fat cream cheese, 1 tsp margarine, and 1 poached egg.

This recipe courtesy of the U.S. Apple Association (www.usapple.org).

French Toast with Poached Plums

Serving Size: 1/4 recipe, **Total Servings:** 4

1/4 cup sugar
1/2 cup water
1 cup plums, any variety, pitted and sliced
1/2 tsp vanilla
1 whole egg and 6 egg whites (or you can use an egg substitute for 4 eggs)
2 Tbsp water or milk
4 1/2-inch thick slices of whole-wheat bread
3 Tbsp canola oil
1/2 tsp confectioner's sugar

1. In a saucepan, combine the sugar and water over medium heat and bring to a boil, stirring until the sugar dissolves. Cook until a thin syrup forms, 4–5 minutes.

2. Add the plums and continue to cook, stirring often, until the plums soften, another 4–5 minutes. Stir in the vanilla. Remove from the heat, cover to keep warm, and set aside.

3. In a shallow baking dish, combine the eggs and water or milk and beat them lightly. Add the bread in a single layer, soaking the first side for 1–2 minutes, then turning and soaking the other side.

4. In a large frying pan, heat the oil. Add the bread and cook until golden, 3–4 minutes. Turn with a spatula and cook the other side until golden, another 3–4 minutes. Put one piece of the bread on each of four plates. Over each, spoon some of the warm plums and their sauce and sprinkle with a little confectioner's sugar. Serve immediately.

EXCHANGES

1 Starch	1 Lean Meat
1 Carbohydrate	1 1/2 Fat

Calories	271
Calories from Fat	114
Total Fat	13 g
Saturated Fat	1.3 g
Polyunsaturated Fat	3.5 g
Monounsaturated Fat	7.1 g
Cholesterol	53 mg
Sodium	247 mg
Total Carbohydrate	31 g
Dietary Fiber	3 g
Sugars	18 g
Protein	10 g

FITTING YOUR PLAN

The carbohydrate exchange is counted as a fruit exchange.

CALORIE PLAN

1500 (borrow 1/2 fat exchange from another meal or snack): 1 serving French Toast with Poached Plums, 1/3 cup baked beans or 1/2 cup oatmeal, and 8 oz nonfat milk.

1800 1 serving French Toast with Poached Plums, 1/3 cup baked beans or 1/2 cup oatmeal, 8 oz nonfat milk, and 3 almonds.

2000 1 serving French Toast with Poached Plums, 1/3 cup baked beans or 1/2 cup oatmeal, 8 oz nonfat milk, and 3 almonds.

This recipe courtesy of the California Tree Fruit Agreement (www.eatcaliforniafruit.com).

Kiwifruit Sweet Omelet

Serving Size: 1/4 recipe, **Total Servings:** 4

3 large California kiwifruit, pared and sliced
4 Tbsp powdered sugar, divided
  Ground cinnamon
3 eggs, separated, and 2 additional egg whites
1/8 tsp salt
1/2 tsp grated lemon peel
1 Tbsp canola oil

1. Sprinkle kiwifruit with 1 Tbsp powdered sugar and a dash of cinnamon in a shallow dish. Let stand 20 minutes; turn occasionally.

2. Beat egg whites and salt until soft peaks form. Gradually add 2 Tbsp powdered sugar; beat until stiff. Beat egg yolks until thick; add lemon peel. Fold into whites.

3. Heat oil in a 10-inch ovenproof skillet (or cover handle of skillet with aluminum foil). Stir in 1 Tbsp powdered sugar and dash cinnamon. Pour in egg mixture; smooth surface. Cook over medium heat for 3–5 minutes or until eggs are puffed and set and bottom is golden brown.

4. Bake at 325°F for 10 minutes or until knife inserted near center comes out clean. Loosen edge of omelet. Make a shallow cut, slightly off center, through top of omelet. Arrange kiwifruit mixture over larger section. Fold smaller portion over kiwifruit. Serve on warm platter. Sprinkle with powdered sugar. Serve hot.

EXCHANGES

1 Fruit	1 Fat	1 Lean Meat

Calories	165
Calories from Fat	67
Total Fat	7 g
Saturated Fat	1.4 g
Polyunsaturated Fat	1.7 g
Monounsaturated Fat	3.5 g
Cholesterol	159 mg
Sodium	158 mg
Total Carbohydrate	18 g
Dietary Fiber	2 g
Sugars	14 g
Protein	7 g

FITTING YOUR PLAN

CALORIE PLAN	
1500	1 serving Kiwifruit Sweet Omelet, 8 oz nonfat milk, and 1 cup oatmeal.
1800	1 serving Kiwifruit Sweet Omelet, 8 oz nonfat milk, 1 cup oatmeal, and 1 tsp margarine.
2000	1 serving Kiwifruit Sweet Omelet, 8 oz nonfat milk, 1 cup oatmeal, and 1 tsp margarine.

This recipe courtesy of the California Kiwifruit Commission (www.kiwifruit.org).

Mushrooms 'n' Eggs on a Muffin

Serving Size: 1 sandwich, **Total Servings:** 2

1 tsp olive oil
8 oz fresh white mushrooms, thinly sliced (about 3 cups)
3 green onions, chopped
2 eggs, beaten
1/8 tsp salt
1 Tbsp grated Parmesan cheese
2 English muffins, split and toasted
2 slices canned, roasted red peppers, well drained

1. In a large skillet (preferably non-stick), heat oil over medium heat.

2. Add mushrooms and onions. Cook and stir until lightly browned, about 5 minutes. Sprinkle with cheese.

3. Cut egg mixture into quarters.

4. Stack two quarters of the egg mixture on the bottom half of each muffin. Top with roasted peppers and muffin tops.

EXCHANGES

2 Starch	1 Medium-Fat Meat
1 Vegetable	1/2 Fat

Calories	278
Calories from Fat	87
Total Fat	10 g
Saturated Fat	2.5 g
Polyunsaturated Fat	1.6 g
Monounsaturated Fat	4 g
Cholesterol	214 mg
Sodium	536 mg
Total Carbohydrate	34 g
Dietary Fiber	4 g
Sugars	5 g
Protein	15 g

FITTING YOUR PLAN

The meal patterns were based on lean-meat exchanges, which have 3 g of fat per ounce. This recipe has a medium-fat exchange, which has 5 g of fat per ounce. Approximately 1/2 extra fat exchange is used in the medium-fat meat.

CALORIE PLAN

1500 (borrow 1 vegetable exchange from dinner): 1 Mushrooms 'n' Eggs on a Muffin sandwich, 8 oz nonfat milk, and 1/2 large grapefruit.

1800 (borrow 1 vegetable exchange from dinner and put 1 fat exchange into another meal): 1 Mushrooms 'n' Eggs on a Muffin sandwich, 8 oz nonfat milk, and 1/2 large grapefruit.

2000 (borrow 1 vegetable exchange from dinner and put 1 fat exchange into another meal): 1 Mushrooms 'n' Eggs on a Muffin sandwich, 8 oz nonfat milk, and 1/2 large grapefruit.

This recipe courtesy of the Mushroom Information Center (www.mushroominfo.com).

Pear-Berry Breakfast Shake

Serving Size: 1/2 recipe, **Total Servings:** 2

1 large Bartlett pear
1 8-oz container of raspberry- or boysenberry-flavored low-fat yogurt
2 Tbsp wheat germ
1/2 cup nonfat milk
1 tsp lemon juice
Egg substitute (pasteurized), amount equivalent to 2 eggs
Dash of salt

1. Combine all ingredients in a blender. Blend until smooth and creamy. Pour into two 12-oz glasses.

EXCHANGES
3 Carbohydrate   1 Very Lean Meat

Calories 239	
Calories from Fat 23	
Total Fat . . . . 3 g	
Saturated Fat . . . . 1.2 g	
Polyunsaturated Fat . . . . 0.5 g	
Monounsaturated Fat . . . . 0.5 g	
Cholesterol . . . . 6 mg	
Sodium . . . . 221 mg	
Total Carbohydrate . . . . 41 g	
Dietary Fiber . . . . 4 g	
Sugars . . . . 31 g	
Protein . . . . 15 g	

FITTING YOUR PLAN

For this meal plan below, the 3 carbohydrate exchanges may be counted as 1 starch, 1 milk, and 1 fruit exchange. You can add 2–3 g of fat because the meat is very lean and the meal plan is based on lean meat. The margarine in the plan below includes this extra fat.

CALORIE PLAN

1500	1 serving Pear-Berry Breakfast Shake, 1/2 cup grits, 1/2 tsp margarine, and 4 pecan halves.
1800	1 serving Pear-Berry Breakfast Shake, 1/2 cup grits, 1/2 tsp margarine, and 8 pecan halves.
2000	1 serving Pear-Berry Breakfast Shake, 1 cup grits, 1/2 tsp margarine, and 8 pecan halves.

This recipe courtesy of the California Pear Advisory Board (www.calpear.com).

Potato and Egg Scramble

Serving Size: 1/4 recipe, **Total Servings:** 4

1 large (8-oz) Idaho potato, peeled and diced
1/4 cup chopped onion
1/4 cup chopped green or red pepper
4 eggs
1/4 cup nonfat milk
1/4 tsp salt
1/8 tsp pepper
Dash of garlic powder

1. Combine potato, onion, and green or red pepper in a 9-inch microwave-safe pie plate. Cover with microwaveable plastic wrap and microwave on high for 4–5 minutes or until potato is tender.

2. Combine eggs, milk, salt, pepper, and garlic powder in a medium bowl; beat slightly.

3. Pour over potatoes in pie plate. Cover with microwaveable plastic wrap and microwave on high for 4 minutes, stirring after 2 minutes. Let stand, covered, for 1 minute. Serve immediately.

EXCHANGES

1 Starch	1 Medium-Fat Meat

Calories 122	
Calories from Fat 46	
Total Fat . . . . 5 g	
Saturated Fat . . . . 1.6 g	
Polyunsaturated Fat . . . . 0.7 g	
Monounsaturated Fat . . . . 1.9 g	
Cholesterol . . . . 212 mg	
Sodium . . . . 225 mg	
Total Carbohydrate . . . . 11 g	
Dietary Fiber . . . . 1 g	
Sugars . . . . 3 g	
Protein . . . . 8 g	

FITTING YOUR PLAN

There is a difference of 2 g of fat between a lean-meat exchange and a medium-fat exchange. Due to this, in the meal plans below you will find 1/2 fat exchange deducted from the plan. The light jam is a free food.

CALORIE PLAN

1500   1 serving Potato and Egg Scramble, 1 slice (1 oz) whole-grain toast, 1 small orange, 8 oz non-fat milk, 1 1/2 tsp low-fat margarine, and 2 tsp light jam.

1800   1 serving Potato and Egg Scramble, 1 slice (1 oz) whole-grain toast, 1 small orange, 8 oz non-fat milk, 1 1/2 tsp tub margarine, 2 tsp light jam, and 6 almonds.

2000   1 serving Potato and Egg Scramble, 1 slice (1 oz) whole-grain toast, 1 small orange, 8 oz non-fat milk, 1 1/2 tsp tub margarine, 2 tsp light jam, and 6 almonds.

This recipe courtesy of the Idaho Potato Commission (www.idahopotato.com).

Strawberry Bran Muffins

Serving Size: 1 muffin, **Total Servings:** 20

3 cups natural bran
1 cup whole-wheat flour
1 cup all-purpose flour
1/2 cup granulated sugar
1 Tbsp baking powder
1 tsp baking soda
2 eggs, beaten
2 cups low-fat buttermilk
1/3 cup canola oil
1/2 cup molasses
1 cup fresh or frozen sliced
  strawberries

1. Preheat oven to 375°F.

2. In a large bowl, mix together the bran, flour, sugar, baking powder, and baking soda.

3. In another bowl, combine the eggs, low-fat buttermilk, canola oil, and molasses; pour into bran mixture and stir just enough to moisten, being careful not to overmix. Fold in strawberries.

4. Spoon into large nonstick or paper-lined muffin tins, filling them almost to the top. Bake for about 25 minutes or until firm to the touch. Remove from oven and let stand for 2 minutes before removing muffins from tin. (This recipe is excellent for freezing. Pop a muffin out of your freezer and warm it in the microwave for a few seconds.)

EXCHANGES

2 Starch   1/2 Fat

Calories 159
    Calories from Fat 46
Total Fat . . . . 5 g
    Saturated Fat . . . . 0.5 g
    Polyunsaturated Fat. . . . . 1.5 g
    Monounsaturated Fat . . . . 2.6 g
Cholesterol . . . . 22 mg
Sodium. . . . . 154 mg
Total Carbohydrate . . . . 29 g
    Dietary Fiber. 6 g
    Sugars . . . . 11 g
Protein . . . . 4 g

FITTING YOUR PLAN

CALORIE PLAN	
1500	1 Strawberry Bran Muffin, 2 scrambled egg whites or low-fat egg substitute, 8 oz nonfat milk, 1 cup cantaloupe, 1 1/2 tsp low-fat margarine, and 1 tsp light jam.
1800	1 Strawberry Bran Muffin, 2 scrambled egg whites or low-fat egg substitute, 8 oz nonfat milk, 1 cup cantaloupe, 1 1/2 tsp margarine, and 1 tsp light jam.
2000	1 Strawberry Bran Muffin, 2 scrambled egg whites or low-fat egg substitute, 8 oz nonfat milk, 1 cup cantaloupe, 1 1/2 tsp margarine, and 1 tsp light jam.

This recipe is courtesy of the Canola Council of Canada (www.canola-council.org).

Strawberry Toast

Serving Size: 2 slices, **Total Servings:** 1

2 slices (1 oz each) whole-grain bread
2 Tbsp fat-free cream cheese
1 1/2 cups California strawberries
1 tsp honey

1. Spread a thin layer of fat-free cream cheese on whole-grain toast. Top with sliced strawberries and drizzle with honey.

EXCHANGES

2 Starch	1/2 Fat	1 Fruit

Calories	256
Calories from Fat	26
Total Fat	3 g
Saturated Fat	0.4 g
Polyunsaturated Fat	0.9 g
Monounsaturated Fat	0.9 g
Cholesterol	4 mg
Sodium	436 mg
Total Carbohydrate	49 g
Dietary Fiber	7 g
Sugars	21 g
Protein	10 g

FITTING YOUR PLAN

CALORIE PLAN	
1500	1 serving Strawberry Toast, 8 oz nonfat milk, 1 egg, and 1/2 tsp margarine.
1800	1 serving Strawberry Toast, 8 oz nonfat milk, 1 egg, 4 pecans, and 1 1/2 tsp margarine.
2000	1 serving Strawberry Toast, 8 oz nonfat milk, 1 egg, 4 pecans, and 1 1/2 tsp margarine.

This recipe courtesy of the California Strawberry Commission (www.calstrawberry.com).

Two-Way Pear Quick Bread

Serving Size: 1 slice, **Total Servings:** 12

1 cup Pear Sauce
1 cup wheat bran flakes cereal
1/3 cup packed brown sugar
1/4 tsp ground cinnamon
1/3 cup oil
1 egg
2 cups flour
1/3 cup raisins
2 tsp baking powder
1/2 tsp salt
1/2 tsp ground nutmeg
1 ripe USA pear, pared, cored, and sliced

TOPPING

1. Combine Pear Sauce and cereal; let stand until sauce is absorbed and add the oil.

2. For the topping, combine 1 Tbsp packed brown sugar and the ground cinnamon. Mix well.

3. Combine the remaining ingredients except the sliced pear and topping. Add the Pear Sauce mixture. Stir only enough to blend.

4. Turn into a greased 8 1/2 X 4 1/2 X 2 1/2-inch loaf pan. Arrange pear slices on batter; sprinkle topping over pears. Bake at 350°F for 70 minutes or until a wooden toothpick inserted near the center comes out clean.

Muffin Variation

Fill 12 greased muffin cups 2/3 full with batter. Bake at 375°F for 30 minutes or until a wooden toothpick inserted in the center comes out clean. Makes 12 muffins.

Pear Sauce

2 ripe medium USA Anjou or Bartlett pears, pared, cored, and sliced
1/2 cup water

Place pears in saucepan with 1/2 cup water and bring to a boil. Simmer, covered, for about 15–20 minutes or until tender. Puree in a blender or food processor. Makes about 2 cups.

EXCHANGES

1 1/2 Starch	1 Fat	1 Fruit

Calories	214
Calories from Fat	63
Total Fat	7 g
Saturated Fat	0.6 g
Polyunsaturated Fat	2.0 g
Monounsaturated Fat	3.9 g
Cholesterol	18 mg
Sodium	203 mg
Total Carbohydrate	36 g
Dietary Fiber	3 g
Sugars	15 g
Protein	3 g

FITTING YOUR PLAN

CALORIE PLAN

1500	(save 1/2 starch exchange for later in the day): 1 serving Two-Way Pear Quick Bread, 8 oz nonfat milk, and 1/4 cup egg substitute (plus nonstick cooking spray for cooking the egg).
1800	(save 1/2 starch exchange for later in the day): 1 serving Two-Way Pear Quick Bread, 8 oz nonfat milk, 1/4 cup egg substitute, and 1 tsp margarine.
2000	(save 1/2 starch exchange for later in the day): 1 serving Two-Way Pear Quick Bread, 8 oz nonfat milk, 1/4 cup egg substitute, and 1 tsp margarine.

This recipe courtesy of Pear Bureau Northwest (www.usapears.com).

Watermelon Blueberry Banana Split

Serving Size: 1/4 recipe, **Total Servings:** 4

2 medium bananas
8 "scoops" watermelon★
1 pint fresh blueberries
1/2 cup low-fat vanilla yogurt
1/4 cup crunchy cereal nuggets

★Use an ice cream scoop to make watermelon balls
(about 1/2 cup each). Remove seeds if needed.

1. Peel bananas and cut in half crosswise; cut each piece in half lengthwise.
For each serving, lay two banana
pieces against sides of shallow dish.
Place watermelon "scoop" at each end
of dish. Fill center space with blueberries. Stir yogurt until smooth; spoon
over watermelon "scoops." Sprinkle
with cereal nuggets.

EXCHANGES

2 1/2 Fruit	1/2 Carbohydrate

Calories 187
  Calories from Fat 16
Total Fat . . . . 2 g
  Saturated Fat . . . . 0.4 g
  Polyunsaturated Fat . . . . 0.5 g
  Monounsaturated Fat . . . . 0.3 g
Cholesterol . . . . 2 mg
Sodium. . . . . 50 mg
Total Carbohydrate . . . . 43 g
  Dietary Fiber. 4 g
  Sugars . . . . 31 g
Protein . . . . 4 g

FITTING YOUR PLAN

This recipe is so good that it's worth borrowing your fruit from other parts of the day. For the meal plans below, the carbohydrate is calculated as 1/2 milk exchange.

CALORIE PLAN

1500   (borrow 1 1/2 fruit exchanges from other meals, but give an extra 4 oz of milk and an extra starch exchange to another meal): 1 serving Watermelon Blueberry Banana Split, 1 plain (1 oz) small roll, 1 oz of cheese with less than 3 g of fat, and 10 peanuts.

1800   (borrow 1 1/2 fruit exchange from other meals, but give an extra 4 oz of milk and an extra starch exchange to another meal): 1 serving Watermelon Blueberry Banana Split, 1 plain (1 oz) small roll, 1 oz of cheese with less than 3 g of fat, and 20 peanuts.

2000   (borrow 1 1/2 fruit exchanges from other meals, but give an extra 4 oz of milk and an extra starch exchange to another meal): 1 serving Watermelon Blueberry Banana Split, 1 plain (1 oz) small roll, 1 oz of cheese with less than 3 g of fat, and 20 peanuts.

This recipe courtesy of the National Watermelon Promotion Board (www.watermelon.org).

Whole-Wheat French Toast with Florida Orange Slices

Serving Size: 1/4 recipe, **Total Servings:** 4

1 large egg
2 large egg whites
1 Tbsp low-fat milk
1 tsp grated orange zest
1/2 tsp vanilla extract
1/8 tsp ground cinnamon
1 Tbsp vegetable oil
4 slices whole-wheat toast
   Florida Orange Slices

1. In a shallow bowl, beat egg, egg whites, milk, orange zest, vanilla extract, and cinnamon until blended.

2. In a large nonstick skillet, heat the oil over medium heat. Dip bread in egg mixture and add to skillet. Cook, turning once, until browned on both sides (3–4 minutes per side). Serve hot with Florida Orange Slices.

Florida Orange Slices

2 small seedless Florida oranges, peeled (white pith removed), halved, and sliced into rounds (not segments)
2 tsp sugar
1/2 tsp vanilla extract

In a small bowl, combine Florida orange slices, sugar, and vanilla extract, tossing to coat. Let stand for 1 hour for flavors to blend.

EXCHANGES

1 Starch	1 Fat	1/2 Fruit

Calories	161
Calories from Fat	53
Total Fat	6 g
Saturated Fat	0.9 g
Polyunsaturated Fat	1.5 g
Monounsaturated Fat	3.0 g
Cholesterol	53 mg
Sodium	194 mg
Total Carbohydrate	21 g
Dietary Fiber	3 g
Sugars	8 g
Protein	7 g

FITTING YOUR PLAN

CALORIE PLAN	
1500	(borrow 1 fat exchange from dinner): 2 servings of Whole-Wheat French Toast with Florida Orange Slices, 6 oz of yogurt with 100 calories or less, and 1 oz low-sodium lean ham.
1800	2 servings of Whole-Wheat French Toast with Florida Orange Slices, 6 oz of yogurt with 100 calories or less, and 1 oz low-sodium lean ham.
2000	2 servings of Whole-Wheat French Toast with Florida Orange Slices, 6 oz of yogurt with 100 calories or less, and 1 oz low-sodium lean ham.

This recipe courtesy of the Florida Department of Citrus (www.floridajuice.com).

Lunch

Almond-Chicken Pear Salad

Serving Size: 1/4 recipe, **Total Servings:** 4

2 cups cooked chicken breasts, cut in 1/2-inch cubes
1/2 cup green pepper, sliced lengthwise
1/4 cup diced celery
1/4 tsp seasoned salt
1/2 cup low-fat plain yogurt
2 Tbsp reduced-calorie mayonnaise
1/2 tsp prepared mustard
1/4 tsp ground ginger
2 ripe medium fresh NW pears (Comice, Anjou, or Bosc), cored and cut into 1-inch cubes
Lettuce
2 Tbsp toasted slivered almonds

1. Toss together chicken, green pepper, and celery. Sprinkle with seasoned salt.

2. Combine yogurt, mayonnaise, mustard, and ginger; add to chicken mixture. Gently mix in pears. Serve on individual lettuce-lined salad plates. Sprinkle with almonds.

EXCHANGES

1 Fruit	1 1/2 Fat	3 Very Lean Meat

Calories 238
    Calories from Fat 70
Total Fat . . . . 8 g
    Saturated Fat . . . . 1.6 g
    Polyunsaturated Fat. . . . . 2.1 g
    Monounsaturated Fat . . . . 3.1 g
Cholesterol . . . . 64 mg
Sodium. . . . . 247 mg
Total Carbohydrate . . . . 18 g
    Dietary Fiber. 4 g
    Sugars . . . . 10 g
Protein . . . . 25 g

FITTING YOUR PLAN

The meal patterns are calculated for lean-meat exchanges. Because the exchanges in this recipe are very-lean-meat exchanges, which have 0–1 g of fat per ounce, and lean meat has 3 g of fat per ounce, you may have an extra 6–9 g of fat (approximately 1 1/2 exchanges) in this calculation.

CALORIE PLAN

1500 (borrow 1 meat exchange from breakfast): 1 serving Almond-Chicken Pear Salad, 3/4 oz whole-wheat crackers (2–5 individual crackers), 1 cup raw sliced tomato, 1 Tbsp salad dressing, and 1 large sugar-free cookie.

1800 (borrow 1 meat exchange from breakfast): 1 serving Almond-Chicken Pear Salad, 3/4 oz whole-wheat crackers (2–5 individual crackers), 1 cup raw sliced tomato, 1 Tbsp salad dressing, 8 large black olives, and 1 large sugar-free cookie.

2000 (borrow 1 meat exchange from breakfast): 1 serving Almond-Chicken Pear Salad, 3/4 oz whole-wheat crackers (2–5 individual crackers), 2 Tbsp raisins, 1 cup raw sliced tomato, 1 Tbsp salad dressing, 1/2 cup cooked spinach, 8 large black olives, and 1 large sugar-free cookie.

This recipe courtesy of Pear Bureau Northwest (www.usapears.com).

Apple-Tortellini Salad

Serving Size: 1 1/3 cups, **Total Servings:** 6

3 Tbsp frozen apple juice concentrate, thawed
3 Tbsp light corn syrup
2 tsp firmly packed brown sugar
1 tsp apple cider vinegar
1/8 tsp garlic salt
    Dash white pepper
1 pkg (9 oz) refrigerated cheese-filled tortellini
2 cups sliced apples
2 cups shredded salad greens
1 cup sliced fresh strawberries
1/2 cup thinly sliced celery
1/4 cup sliced green onions
2 Tbsp pine nuts, toasted (*optional*)

1. Combine apple juice concentrate, corn syrup, brown sugar, vinegar, garlic salt, and pepper. Cover dressing and refrigerate.

2. Cook tortellini according to package directions. Drain and cool thoroughly. In a large mixing bowl, combine tortellini and remaining ingredients. Toss gently with apple juice dressing and serve immediately.

EXCHANGES

1 1/2 Starch	1/2 Fat	1 Fruit

Calories 209
    Calories from Fat 27
Total Fat . . . . 3 g
    Saturated Fat . . . . 1.4 g
    Polyunsaturated Fat . . . . 0.7 g
    Monounsaturated Fat . . . . 0.6 g
Cholesterol. . . . . 16 mg
Sodium. . . . . 247 mg
Total Carbohydrate . . . . 41 g
    Dietary Fiber. 3 g
    Sugars . . . . 17 g
Protein . . . . 7 g

FITTING YOUR PLAN

CALORIE PLAN	
1500	1 serving Apple-Tortellini Salad, 2 slices Melba toast, 2 oz lean meat, 1/2 cup tomato or vegetable juice, and 1 1/2 tsp reduced-fat mayonnaise.
1800	1 serving Apple-Tortellini Salad, 2 slices Melba toast, 2 oz lean meat, 1/2 cup vegetable juice, 1 1/2 tsp reduced-fat mayonnaise, and 4 pecan halves.
2000	1 serving Apple-Tortellini Salad, 1 small apple, 2 slices Melba toast, 2 oz lean meat, 1 cup tomato or vegetable juice, 1 1/2 tsp reduced-fat mayonnaise, and 4 pecan halves.

This recipe courtesy of the U.S. Apple Association (www.usapple.org).

Basil Tomato Salad

Serving Size: 1/6 recipe, **Total Servings:** 6

2 Tbsp olive oil
2 Tbsp cider vinegar
2 tsp chopped fresh basil leaves
  (or 1 tsp dried basil)
1/2 tsp salt
1/4 tsp ground black pepper
3 cups cooked rice, cooled
2 medium tomatoes, chopped
1 medium cucumber, peeled,
  seeded, and chopped
1 small red onion, chopped

1. Whisk together oil, vinegar, basil, salt, and pepper in a large bowl. Add rice, tomatoes, cucumber, and onion; toss. Serve chilled.

EXCHANGES

1 1/2 Starch	1/2 Fat	1 Vegetable

Calories 160	
Calories from Fat 44	
Total Fat . . . . 5 g	
Saturated Fat . . . . 0.7 g	
Polyunsaturated Fat . . . . 0.5 g	
Monounsaturated Fat . . . . 3.4 g	
Cholesterol . . . . 0 mg	
Sodium. . . . . 199 mg	
Total Carbohydrate . . . . 26 g	
Dietary Fiber. . . . . 1 g	
Sugars . . . . 2 g	
Protein . . . . 3 g	

FITTING YOUR PLAN

CALORIE PLAN	
1500	1 serving Basil Tomato Salad, 1 1/2 cup fat-free popcorn, 1 1/2 tsp low-fat margarine, 3/4 cup blackberries, and 2 oz lean meat.
1800	1 serving Basil Tomato Salad, 1 1/2 cups fat-free popcorn, 1 1/2 tsp low-fat margarine, 3/4 cup blackberries, 2 oz lean meat, and 8 large black olives.
2000	1 serving Basil Tomato Salad, 1 1/2 cups fat-free popcorn, 1 1/2 tsp low-fat margarine, 3/4 cup blackberries, 4 oz banana, 1 cup raw nonstarchy vegetables, 2 oz lean meat, and 8 large black olives.

This recipe courtesy of the U.S.A. Rice Federation (www.usarice.com).

Bay Area Classic Ham Sandwich

Serving Size: 1 sandwich, **Total Servings:** 2

4 slices sourdough bread (1 oz each)

2 Tbsp fat-free cream cheese

4 slices (4 oz) very lean ham, sliced thin

1/2 cup lettuce, shredded

2 Roma tomatoes, sliced thin

2 Tbsp sliced banana peppers

1. Toast bread; spread one side of each slice with cream cheese. Layer ham on two slices of bread. Top with lettuce, tomatoes, and banana peppers; add remaining bread. Cut each sandwich in half and serve.

EXCHANGES

2 Starch	2 Very Lean Meat	1 Vegetable

Calories	252
Calories from Fat	28
Total Fat	3 g
Saturated Fat	0.8 g
Polyunsaturated Fat	0.7 g
Monounsaturated Fat	1.1 g
Cholesterol	28 mg
Sodium	906 mg
Total Carbohydrate	37 g
Dietary Fiber	3 g
Sugars	5 g
Protein	19 g

FITTING YOUR PLAN

Because this recipe has 2 very-lean-meat exchanges, you get an extra 5–6 g of fat for the day, which equals an extra fat exchange.

CALORIE PLAN

1500	1 serving Bay Area Classic Ham Sandwich, 1 medium peach, and 12 mixed nuts.
1800	1 serving Bay Area Classic Ham Sandwich, 1 medium peach, and 18 mixed nuts.
2000	1 serving Bay Area Classic Ham Sandwich, 1 large peach, 1/2 cup cooked Brussels sprouts, and 18 mixed nuts.

This recipe courtesy of the National Pork Board (www.porkandhealth.org).

Beef and Broccoli with Walnuts*

Serving Size: 1/6 recipe, **Total Servings:** 6

1/2 cup walnut halves
  4 Tbsp plum jelly or fruit spread
  1 Tbsp water
  1 pkg (1 lb) fully cooked beef pot
    roast with gravy
1/2 cup Chinese-style Hoisin sauce
  2 cups instant rice, cooked
  3 cups fresh broccoli florets, cooked

1. Heat a large nonstick skillet over medium heat until hot. Combine walnuts, 2 Tbsp plum jelly, and water in skillet. Cook and stir continuously for 5 minutes or until walnuts are slightly glazed. Transfer to plate; spread to separate.

2. Remove beef pot roast from package. Measure 3/4 cup of the gravy and place gravy in same skillet. (Add beef broth or water to equal 3/4 cup if necessary.)

3. Add 1/2 cup Hoisin sauce and 2 Tbsp plum jelly to skillet. Heat over medium heat until hot, stirring occasionally.

4. Cut pot roast into 1-inch pieces; add to skillet. Cook over medium-low heat for 5–6 minutes or until beef is heated thoroughly, stirring occasionally.

5. Spoon beef mixture and walnuts over cooked rice and broccoli.

EXCHANGES

1 Starch	2 Lean Meat
1 Carbohydrate	1/2 Fat

Calories 291
  Calories from Fat 85
Total Fat . . . . 9 g
  Saturated Fat . . . . 1.5 g
  Polyunsaturated Fat . . . . 4.8 g
  Monounsaturated Fat . . . . 0.9 g
Cholesterol . . . . 40 mg
Sodium . . . . 844 mg
Total Carbohydrate . . . . 32 g
  Dietary Fiber. 3 g
  Sugars . . . . 15 g
Protein . . . . 19 g

*This recipe is relatively high in sodium. Adjust your meals throughout the day to accommodate this.

FITTING YOUR PLAN

The carbohydrate exchange is counted as a starch exchange in this meal pattern.

CALORIE PLAN

1500   1 serving Beef and Broccoli with Walnuts, 1 cup mixed salad made with nonstarchy vegetables, 1/2 tsp olive oil with vinegar to taste, and 1 small apple.

1800   1 serving Beef and Broccoli with Walnuts, 1 small apple, 1 cup mixed salad made with nonstarchy vegetables, and 1 1/2 tsp olive oil with vinegar to taste.

2000   1 serving Beef and Broccoli with Walnuts, 1 large apple (8 oz), 2 cups mixed salad made with nonstarchy vegetables, and 1 1/2 tsp olive oil with vinegar to taste.

This recipe courtesy of the Texas Beef Council (www.txbeef.org).

California Guacamole

Serving Size: 1/12 recipe, **Total Servings:** 12

2 medium California avocados
3 Tbsp fresh lemon juice
1/2 cup onion, diced
3 Tbsp tomato, chopped
1/2 tsp salt
2 Tbsp cilantro, minced

1. Cut the avocados in half and remove the seeds.

2. Scoop out the pulp and place in a bowl.

3. Drizzle the pulp with lemon juice and mash.

4. Combine with the remaining ingredients, mix well, and serve.

EXCHANGES
1 Fat

Calories 58
    Calories from Fat 46
Total Fat . . . . 5 g
    Saturated Fat . . . . 0.8 g
    Polyunsaturated Fat . . . . 0.7 g
    Monounsaturated Fat . . . . 3.2 g
Cholesterol . . . . 0 mg
Sodium . . . . 101 mg
Total Carbohydrate . . . . 3 g
    Dietary Fiber . . . . 2 g
    Sugars . . . . 1 g
Protein . . . . 1 g

FITTING YOUR PLAN

CALORIE PLAN	
1500	1 serving California Guacamole (mix with 2 oz canned tuna packed in water), 2 slices (1 oz each) whole-wheat bread, 1 small banana (4 oz), and 1 cup raw nonstarchy vegetables.
1800	2 servings California Guacamole (mix with 2 oz canned tuna packed in water), 2 slices (1 oz each) whole-wheat bread, 1 small banana (4 oz), and 1 cup raw nonstarchy vegetables.
2000	2 servings California Guacamole (mix with 2 oz canned tuna packed in water), 2 slices (1 oz each) whole-wheat bread, 1 large banana (8 oz), and 2 cups raw nonstarchy vegetables.

This recipe courtesy of the California Avocado Commission (www.avocado.org).

Citrus Olive Crab Salad

Serving Size: 1 cup crab-citrus mixture **Total Servings:** 4
(plus 2 cups lettuce)

3/4 cup California ripe olives, wedged
1/2 cup yellow grapefruit segments
1/2 cup red onion, sliced into thin strips
1/2 cup cucumber, peeled, seeded, and diced
1/3 cup ruby grapefruit segments
1/3 cup orange segments
1/4 cup tangerine segments
2 Tbsp basil, chopped
2 Tbsp cilantro, chopped
1 Tbsp red wine vinegar
1/4 tsp salt
6 oz crab meat
1/2 cup avocado, diced into 1/2-inch cubes
8 cups butter lettuce leaves

1. In a large mixing bowl, combine the olives, yellow grapefruit, onion, cucumber, ruby grapefruit, orange, and tangerine. Season with basil, cilantro, vinegar, and salt. Add crab and avocado and gently toss until evenly combined. To serve, divide lettuce onto each plate and top with the citrus crab mixture.

EXCHANGES

1/2 Fruit	1 Very Lean Meat
1 Vegetable	1 1/2 Fat

Calories	156
Calories from Fat	58
Total Fat	6 g
Saturated Fat	0.9 g
Polyunsaturated Fat	1.1 g
Monounsaturated Fat	3.7 g
Cholesterol	42 mg
Sodium	499 mg
Total Carbohydrate	16 g
Dietary Fiber	5 g
Sugars	8 g
Protein	11 g

FITTING YOUR PLAN

This recipe uses very lean meat; therefore, an extra 2–3 g of fat or 1/2 fat exchange may be added to a meal. The lima beans below are counted as 1 starch and 1 very-lean-meat exchange; therefore, 2–3 g of fat or 1/2 fat exchange may be added to this meal.

CALORIE PLAN

1500 (save 1/2 fruit exchange to add to another meal): 1 serving Citrus Olive Crab Salad, 2/3 cup lima beans, and 3/4 oz (3 individual) whole-wheat crackers.

1800 (save 1/2 fruit exchange to add to another meal): 1 serving Citrus Olive Crab Salad, 2/3 cup lima beans, 3/4 oz (3 individual) whole-wheat crackers, and 6 walnut halves.

2000 (save 1/2 fruit exchange to add to another meal): 1 serving Citrus Olive Crab Salad, 2/3 cup lima beans mixed with 1/2 cup canned tomatoes, 3/4 oz (3 individual) whole-wheat crackers, 6 walnut halves, and a kiwi.

This recipe courtesy of the California Olive Industry (www.californiaolives.org).

Citrus Slaw

Serving Size: 1/6 recipe, **Total Servings:** 6

1/4 cup prepared nonfat herb vinaigrette

1/4 cup frozen orange juice concentrate, thawed

4 cups Napa cabbage, shredded

2 medium oranges, peeled and segmented

1 medium red apple, halved, cored, and diced

1 cup (about 6 oz) pitted dried plums, quartered

1/2 cup celery, sliced

1/4 cup green onions, sliced
Pepper (*optional*)

1. In large bowl, whisk together vinaigrette and juice concentrate. Add cabbage, oranges, apple, dried plums, celery, and green onions, tossing to coat. Season with pepper, if desired.

EXCHANGES
2 Fruit   1 Vegetable

Calories 144
  Calories from Fat 3
Total Fat . . . . 0 g
  Saturated Fat . . . . 0.0 g
  Polyunsaturated Fat. . . . . 0.1 g
  Monounsaturated Fat . . . . 0.1 g
Cholesterol . . . . 0 mg
Sodium. . . . . 120 mg
Total Carbohydrate . . . . 36 g
  Dietary Fiber. 5 g
  Sugars . . . . 26 g
Protein . . . . 2 g

FITTING YOUR PLAN

CALORIE PLAN

1500 (borrow 1 fruit exchange from breakfast): 1 serving Citrus Slaw, 2 slices whole-grain bread, 2 oz lean meat or fish, lettuce in sandwich, and 1 Tbsp reduced-fat mayonnaise.

1800 (borrow 1 fruit exchange from snack): 1 serving Citrus Slaw, 2 slices whole-grain bread, 2 oz lean meat or fish, lettuce in sandwich, 1 Tbsp reduced-fat mayonnaise, and 4 pecan halves.

2000 1 serving Citrus Slaw, 2 slices whole-grain bread, 1/2 cup red beets, 2 oz lean meat or fish, lettuce in sandwich, 1 Tbsp reduced-fat mayonnaise, and 4 pecan halves.

This recipe courtesy of the California Dried Plum Board (www.californiadriedplums.org).

Colorful Chickpea Salad

Serving Size: 1/4 recipe, **Total Servings:** 4

1 large carrot, sliced
1 medium potato, peeled and cubed
1/2 cup peas, fresh or frozen
2 cups USA chickpeas, cooked or canned
2 tsp olive oil
1 large onion, sliced
4 cloves garlic, minced
1 oz mild reduced-fat cheddar cheese, cut into 1/3-inch cubes
1 oz reduced-fat Colby cheese, cut into 1/3-inch cubes
2 Tbsp red wine vinegar
1 1/2 tsp dried dill weed
Salt and freshly ground pepper to taste

1. Place the carrot in a saucepan with enough water to cover plus 1 inch. Bring to a boil, reduce the heat to medium low, and cook the carrot for 5 minutes.

2. Add the potato and peas (if fresh) and cook for another 10 minutes. If you are using frozen peas, add them during the last 2 minutes of cooking time.

3. Remove the pan from the heat, and add the chickpeas, tossing to warm them.

4. Meanwhile, heat the oil in a small skillet. Sauté the onion and garlic until they are just tender. Do not let them brown.

5. Drain the chickpea mixture and transfer it to a serving bowl. Add the onion-garlic mixture and the cheese. Add the vinegar, dill, salt, and a generous amount of freshly ground pepper. Toss the ingredients lightly to combine them well. Serve the salad warm or cold.

EXCHANGES

2 Starch	1 Lean Meat
2 Vegetable	1/2 Fat

Calories	271
Calories from Fat	67
Total Fat	7 g
Saturated Fat	2.3 g
Polyunsaturated Fat	1.3 g
Monounsaturated Fat	3.0 g
Cholesterol	10 mg
Sodium	155 mg
Total Carbohydrate	40 g
Dietary Fiber	10 g
Sugars	12 g
Protein	14 g

FITTING YOUR PLAN

CALORIE PLAN	
1500	(borrow 1 vegetable exchange from snack): 1 serving Colorful Chickpea Salad, 1 oz of cheese that is 3 g of fat per ounce or less, 1/2 cup canned apricots in extra-light syrup, and 3 mixed nuts.
1800	(borrow 1 vegetable exchange from snack): 1 serving Colorful Chickpea Salad, 1 oz of cheese that is 3 g of fat per ounce or less, 1/2 cup canned apricots in extra-light syrup, and 9 mixed nuts.
2000	1 serving Colorful Chickpea Salad, 1 oz of cheese that is 3 g of fat per ounce or less, 1 cup canned apricots in extra-light syrup, and 9 mixed nuts.

This recipe courtesy of the U.S.A. Dry Pea & Lentil Council (www.pea-lentil.com).

Couscous Salad with Dried Cherries

Serving Size: 1/6 recipe, **Total Servings:** 6

1 cup water or fat-free, reduced-sodium chicken broth

3/4 cup quick-cooking couscous, uncooked

1/2 cup dried tart cherries

1/2 cup carrots, coarsely chopped

1/2 cup cucumber, chopped, unpeeled

1/4 cup green onions, sliced

1/4 cup toasted pine nuts or slivered almonds (*optional*)★

3 Tbsp balsamic vinegar

1 Tbsp olive oil

1 Tbsp Dijon-style mustard

Salt and pepper, to taste

★To toast pine nuts or almonds, spread the nuts in an ungreased pan. Bake in a preheated 350°F oven for 5–7 minutes, stirring occasionally, or until brown.

1. Bring water or broth to a boil in a medium saucepan; stir in couscous. Remove from heat; let stand, covered, 5 minutes. Fluff with a fork. Uncover; let cool 10 minutes.

2. Put cooked couscous, dried cherries, carrots, cucumber, green onions, and pine nuts in a large bowl; mix well.

3. Combine vinegar, olive oil, and mustard in a small container; mix well. Pour over couscous mixture; stir to coat all ingredients. Season with salt and pepper, if desired. Serve chilled or at room temperature.

EXCHANGES

1 Starch	1 Vegetable
1/2 Fruit	1/2 Fat

Calories	154
Calories from Fat	23
Total Fat	3 g
Saturated Fat	0.3 g
Polyunsaturated Fat	0.3 g
Monounsaturated Fat	1.7 g
Cholesterol	0 mg
Sodium	156 mg
Total Carbohydrate	29 g
Dietary Fiber	2 g
Sugars	9 g
Protein	4 g

FITTING YOUR PLAN

CALORIE PLAN	
1500	(save 1/2 fruit exchange for another meal): 1 serving Couscous Salad with Dried Cherries; 2 oz lean chicken, turkey, beef, seafood, or pork; 1 pumpernickel roll (1 oz); and 1 1/2 tsp low-fat margarine.
1800	(save 1/2 fruit exchange for another meal): 1 serving Couscous Salad with Dried Cherries; 2 oz lean chicken, turkey, beef, seafood, or pork; 1 pumpernickel roll (1 oz); 1 1/2 tsp low-fat margarine; and 1 Tbsp pumpkin seeds.
2000	1 serving Couscous Salad with Dried Cherries; 2 oz lean chicken, turkey, beef, seafood, or pork; 1 pumpernickel roll (1 oz); 1 1/2 tsp low-fat margarine; 1 Tbsp pumpkin seeds; 3/4 cup canned pears in extra-light syrup; and 1/2 cup artichoke hearts.

This recipe courtesy of the Cherry Marketing Institute (www.usacherries.com).

Creamy Smoked Turkey and Blueberry Salad

Serving Size: 1 cup, **Total Servings:** 8

1/2 cup light mayonnaise
1/2 cup plain low-fat yogurt
1/4 cup orange marmalade
  2 tsp fresh lemon juice
1/2 tsp ground black pepper
  3 medium peaches (about 1 lb),
    cut in wedges (about 3 cups)
  1 pint blueberries
  2 cups cubed smoked turkey
    (about 8 oz)

1. In a bowl, combine mayonnaise, yogurt, marmalade, lemon juice, and pepper. Add peach slices, blueberries, and turkey; toss until well coated. Serve on lettuce leaves, if desired.

EXCHANGES

1/2 Fruit	1 Very Lean Meat
1/2 Carbohydrate	1 Fat

Calories	154
Calories from Fat	51
Total Fat	6 g
Saturated Fat	1.2 g
Polyunsaturated Fat	2.2 g
Monounsaturated Fat	1.5 g
Cholesterol	21 mg
Sodium	416 mg
Total Carbohydrate	19 g
Dietary Fiber	2 g
Sugars	13 g
Protein	7 g

FITTING YOUR PLAN

This meal pattern is based on lean-meat exchanges, so you can have an extra 2–3 g of fat (1/2 fat exchange) in this calculation. The 1/2 carbohydrate exchange is counted below as 1/2 fruit exchange.

CALORIE PLAN

1500   1 serving Creamy Smoked Turkey and Blueberry Salad, 1/2 cup corn, 4 no-fat-added whole-wheat crackers (3/4 oz), 1/2 cup cooked broccoli, 1 oz low-fat cheese, and 5 peanuts.

1800   1 serving Creamy Smoked Turkey and Blueberry Salad, 1/2 cup corn, 4 no-fat-added whole-wheat crackers (3/4 oz), 1/2 cup cooked broccoli, 1 oz low-fat cheese, and 15 peanuts.

2000   (save 1 fruit exchange for another meal): 1 serving Creamy Smoked Turkey and Blueberry Salad, 1/2 cup corn, 4 no-fat-added whole-wheat crackers (3/4 oz), 1 cup cooked broccoli, 1 oz low-fat cheese, and 15 peanuts.

This recipe courtesy of the U.S. Highbush Blueberry Council (www.ushbc.org).

Egg-White Omelet with Spinach or Chard

Serving Size: 1 omelet, **Total Servings:** 1

2 tsp olive oil
2 cups spinach or chard leaves
Salt and pepper (freshly milled)
3 egg whites, beaten with 1/2 tsp chopped marjoram or chives

1. In a small nonstick skillet, heat 1 tsp of oil, add the spinach or chard, and cook until wilted. Season with salt and pepper, then transfer to a plate.

2. Add the second teaspoon of oil to the pan, then pour in the egg whites. Tilt the pan to spread them out; cook over medium heat until the eggs set. Season with a pinch of salt and pepper, arrange the spinach over 1/3 of the eggs, then gently prod the eggs over it to make a rolled omelet.

EXCHANGES

2 Very Lean Meat	1 1/2 Fat

Calories 145
    Calories from Fat 83
Total Fat . . . . 9 g
    Saturated Fat . . . . 1.2 g
    Polyunsaturated Fat . . . . 0.8 g
    Monounsaturated Fat . . . . 6.6 g
Cholesterol . . . . 0 mg
Sodium . . . . 213 mg
Total Carbohydrate . . . . 3 g
    Dietary Fiber . . . . 2 g
    Sugars . . . . 1 g
Protein . . . . 12 g

FITTING YOUR PLAN

This meal plan is based on lean-meat exchanges, so you can have an extra 4–6 g of fat (1 fat exchange) in this calculation due to the 2 very-lean-meat exchanges.

CALORIE PLAN

1500   1 serving Egg-White Omelet with Spinach or Chard, 1/2 bagel (2 oz), 3/4 cup mixed blueberries and honeydew melon, 1/2 cup mixed cooked okra and tomatoes, 2 tsp light jam, and 1 1/2 tsp low-fat margarine.

1800   1 serving Egg-White Omelet with Spinach or Chard, 1/2 bagel (2 oz), 3/4 cup mixed blueberries and honeydew melon, 1/2 cup mixed cooked okra and tomatoes, 2 tsp light jam, and 1 1/2 tsp soft margarine.

2000   1 serving Egg-White Omelet with Spinach or Chard, 1/2 bagel (2 oz), 1 1/2 cups mixed blueberries and honeydew melon, 1 cup mixed cooked okra and tomatoes, 2 tsp light jam, and 1 1/2 tsp soft margarine.

This recipe courtesy of the Leafy Greens Council (www.leafy-greens.org).

Fresh Sweet Corn and Mozzarella Salad

Serving Size: 1/2 cup, **Total Servings:** 10

4 large ears fresh sweet corn, husked
1 cup sliced celery
4 oz cubed low-fat mozzarella cheese (smoked, if possible)
1/2 cup diced sweet red bell pepper
1/2 cup sliced black olives
1/3 cup bottled fat-free Italian dressing

1. With a sharp knife, cut kernels from sweet corn cobs (makes about 3 cups). In a large bowl, combine corn kernels, celery, cheese, red pepper, and black olives. Add Italian dressing; toss until well coated. Serve as a side dish or on lettuce leaves.

EXCHANGES
1 Starch   1/2 Fat

Calories	95
Calories from Fat	24
Total Fat	3 g
Saturated Fat	1.2 g
Polyunsaturated Fat	0.4 g
Monounsaturated Fat	0.9 g
Cholesterol	6 mg
Sodium	235 mg
Total Carbohydrate	15 g
Dietary Fiber	2 g
Sugars	3 g
Protein	5 g

FITTING YOUR PLAN

CALORIE PLAN

1500 1 serving Fresh Sweet Corn and Mozzarella Salad, 1 slice (1 oz) whole-grain bread, 1 cup honeydew melon, 1 cup raw carrot sticks, 2 oz lean meat, mustard, and 1 1/2 tsp sunflower seeds.

1800 1 serving Fresh Sweet Corn and Mozzarella Salad, 1 slice (1 oz) whole-grain bread, 1 cup honeydew melon, 1 cup raw carrot sticks, 2 oz lean meat, mustard, 1 1/2 Tbsp sunflower seeds.

2000 1 serving Fresh Sweet Corn and Mozzarella Salad, 1 slice (1 oz) whole-grain bread, 2 cups honeydew melon, 2 cups raw carrot sticks, 2 oz lean meat, mustard, and 1 1/2 Tbsp sunflower seeds.

This recipe courtesy of the Fresh Super Sweet Corn Council (www.freshsupersweetcorn.com).

Fruited Carrots

Serving Size: 1/4 recipe, **Total Servings:** 4

1 lb carrots, julienned
2 Tbsp low-saturated-fat margarine
1 1/2 tsp cornstarch
1/2 cup orange juice
1/4 tsp salt
1 cup fresh Bartlett pears, sliced or chopped

1. Stir-fry the carrots in the margarine until crisp tender.

2. Combine cornstarch with orange juice and salt. Stir into carrots and cook, uncovered, until sauce is thickened.

3. Add pears; toss gently. Serve warm.

EXCHANGES

1/2 Fruit   1 Fat   3 Vegetable

Calories	139
Calories from Fat	54
Total Fat	6 g
Saturated Fat	1.1 g
Polyunsaturated Fat	1.9 g
Monounsaturated Fat	2.6 g
Cholesterol	0 mg
Sodium	282 mg
Total Carbohydrate	21 g
Dietary Fiber	5 g
Sugars	12 g
Protein	2 g

FITTING YOUR PLAN

CALORIE PLAN	
1500	(1/2 fruit exchange may be used for another meal, borrow 1 vegetable exchange from snack and 1 from dinner): 1 serving Fruited Carrots; 2 oz lean chicken, fish, beef, or pork; and 2/3 cup baked beans.
1800	(1/2 fruit exchange may be used for another meal, borrow 1 vegetable exchange from snack and 1 from dinner): 1 serving Fruited Carrots; 2 oz lean chicken, fish, beef, or pork; 2/3 cup baked beans; and 10 peanuts.
2000	(borrow 1 vegetable exchange from snack or dinner): 1 serving Fruited Carrots; 2 oz lean chicken, fish, beef, or pork; 2/3 cup baked beans; 10 peanuts; and 3/4 of a large Bartlett pear.

This recipe courtesy of the California Pear Advisory Board (www.calpear.com).

Garden Vegetable Pistachio Potato Salad

Serving Size: 1/12 recipe, **Total Servings:** 12

2 lb new red potatoes
1 cup petite frozen peas, defrosted*
1 large carrot, pared, sliced (1 cup)
1 cup fresh corn kernels (2 ears)
1 cup broccoli florets, cut into small pieces
1/4 cup green onion, sliced
1/2 cup California pistachios
3/4 cup plain nonfat yogurt
3/4 cup fat-free mayonnaise
1 tsp dill weed
1/2 tsp black pepper

*To thaw peas, pour hot water from cooking potatoes over peas in a sieve.

1. Cook whole potatoes in boiling water, about 15–20 minutes or until tender; drain. Cool; then slice potatoes into 1/4-inch thick pieces. Combine potatoes with peas, carrot, corn, broccoli, green onion, and pistachios in a large bowl. Stir the yogurt with mayonnaise, dill, and pepper; combine with vegetables and toss gently.

EXCHANGES
2 Starch

Calories 146
  Calories from Fat 25
Total Fat . . . . 3 g
  Saturated Fat . . . . 0.4 g
  Polyunsaturated Fat . . . . 0.9 g
  Monounsaturated Fat . . . . 1.3 g
Cholesterol . . . . 0 mg
Sodium . . . . 161 mg
Total Carbohydrate . . . . 26 g
  Dietary Fiber . . . . 4 g
  Sugars . . . . 5 g
Protein . . . . 5 g

FITTING YOUR PLAN

CALORIE PLAN

1500 1 serving Garden Vegetable Pistachio Potato Salad, 2 oz fresh salmon or other lean meat, 1/2 cup canned sweet cherries packed in extra-light syrup or no sugar added, 1/2 cup cooked greens, and 1 tsp margarine.

1800 1 serving Garden Vegetable Pistachio Potato Salad, 2 oz fresh salmon or other lean meat, 1/2 cup canned sweet cherries packed in extra-light syrup or no sugar added, 1/2 cup cooked greens, and 2 tsp margarine.

2000 1 serving Garden Vegetable Pistachio Potato Salad, 2 oz fresh salmon or other lean meat, 1 cup canned sweet cherries packed in extra-light syrup or no sugar added, 1 cup cooked greens, and 2 tsp margarine.

This recipe courtesy of the California Pistachio Commission (www.pistachios.org).

Great Meatloaf

Serving Size: 1/10 recipe, **Total Servings:** 10

2 lb ground turkey
2 egg whites, slightly beaten
1 cup bread crumbs
1/4 cup onion, chopped
1/4 cup nonfat milk
2 tsp horseradish
1 tsp dry mustard
3/4 cup catsup

1. Combine all ingredients; form into a loaf. Bake in oven at 350°F for 1 hour. (Can be cooked in a microwave: cook uncovered on high power for 12–14 minutes; let stand 5–10 minutes.)

EXCHANGES

1/2 Starch	3 Lean Meat	1 Vegetable

Calories	225
Calories from Fat	85
Total Fat	9 g
Saturated Fat	2.2 g
Polyunsaturated Fat	2.3 g
Monounsaturated Fat	3.4 g
Cholesterol	67 mg
Sodium	393 mg
Total Carbohydrate	14 g
Dietary Fiber	1 g
Sugars	3 g
Protein	21 g

FITTING YOUR PLAN

CALORIE PLAN	
1500	(borrow 1 meat exchange from breakfast): 1 serving Great Meatloaf, 3/4 cup mashed potatoes, 1/2 cup unsweetened applesauce, and 1 tsp margarine.
1800	(borrow 1 meat exchange from breakfast): 1 serving Great Meatloaf, 3/4 cup mashed potatoes, 1/2 cup unsweetened applesauce, and 2 tsp margarine.
2000	(borrow 1 meat exchange from breakfast): 1 serving Great Meatloaf, 3/4 cup mashed potatoes, 1 cup unsweetened applesauce, 1/2 cup cooked green beans, and 2 tsp margarine.

This recipe courtesy of the Horseradish Information Council (www.horseradish.org).

Green Beans with Garlic, Prosciutto, and Olives

Serving Size: 1/6 recipe, **Total Servings:** 6

1/4–1/2 oz prosciutto or bacon, finely chopped
2 cloves garlic, minced
1 Tbsp olive oil
1 lb slender green beans, ends trimmed
1/3 cup water
1 1/2 tsp Fresh rosemary (1/2 tsp dried)
3/4 cup California ripe olives, wedges
Pepper to taste

1. Add prosciutto and garlic to hot oil in frying pan. Cook, stirring, just until prosciutto is crisp (do not scorch), for about 2 minutes. Quickly remove prosciutto and garlic from pan with slotted spoon and set aside.

2. Add beans, water, and rosemary to pan. Cover and cook until beans are just tender to bite, about 5 minutes. Gently mix in olives.

3. Cook, uncovered, stirring occasionally, until most of the liquid has evaporated, 3–4 minutes. Transfer bean mixture to a serving bowl and sprinkle with prosciutto and garlic. Garnish with pepper to taste.

EXCHANGES
1 Vegetable   1 Fat

Calories	65
Calories from Fat	39
Total Fat	4 g
Saturated Fat	0.7 g
Polyunsaturated Fat	0.4 g
Monounsaturated Fat	2.9 g
Cholesterol	1 mg
Sodium	180 mg
Total Carbohydrate	6 g
Dietary Fiber	3 g
Sugars	1 g
Protein	2 g

FITTING YOUR PLAN

CALORIE PLAN	
1500	1 serving Green Beans with Garlic, Prosciutto, and Olives, 2 slices (1 oz each) whole-grain bread, 4 fresh apricots, 2 oz lean meat, lettuce, and 1 tsp reduced-fat mayonnaise.
1800	1 serving Green Beans with Garlic, Prosciutto, and Olives, 2 slices (1 oz each) whole-grain bread, 4 fresh apricots, 2 oz lean meat, lettuce, 1 tsp reduced-fat mayonnaise, and 6 mixed nuts.
2000	1 serving Green Beans with Garlic, Prosciutto, and Olives, 2 slices (1 oz each) whole-grain bread, 4 fresh apricots, 1 small orange, 2 oz lean meat, lettuce, 1 tsp reduced-fat mayonnaise, 6 mixed nuts, and 1 cup raw nonstarchy vegetables.

This recipe courtesy of the California Olive Industry (www.californiaolives.org).

Hearty Chicken and Rice Soup

Serving Size: 1/8 recipe, **Total Servings:** 8

1 cup onion, chopped
1 cup celery, sliced
1 cup carrots, sliced
3/4 cup uncooked rice
1/4 cup chopped fresh parsley
1/2 tsp cracked black pepper
1/2 tsp dried thyme leaves
1 bay leaf
10 cups fat-free, reduced-sodium chicken broth
1 1/2 cups (about 3/4 lb) chicken cubes, cut in 3/4-inch pieces
2 Tbsp fresh lime juice

1. Combine onion, celery, carrots, rice, parsley, pepper, thyme, bay leaf, and chicken broth in a Dutch oven. Bring to a boil; stir once or twice. Simmer uncovered 20 minutes.

2. Add chicken cubes; simmer uncovered 5–10 minutes or until chicken is cooked. Remove bay leaf. Stir in lime juice just before serving.

EXCHANGES

1 Starch	1 Lean Meat	1 Vegetable

Calories 163
 Calories from Fat 26
Total Fat . . . . 3 g
 Saturated Fat . . . . 0.7 g
 Polyunsaturated Fat . . . . 0.7 g
 Monounsaturated Fat . . . . 0.9 g
Cholesterol . . . . 27 mg
Sodium . . . . 686 mg
Total Carbohydrate . . . . 19 g
 Dietary Fiber . . . . 1 g
 Sugars . . . . 3 g
Protein . . . . 14 g

FITTING YOUR PLAN

CALORIE PLAN	
1500	1 serving Hearty Chicken and Rice Soup, 2 rice cakes (4 inches across), 1 oz cheese with less than 3 g of fat, 8 large black olives, and 1/2 small mango fruit.
1800	1 serving Hearty Chicken and Rice Soup, 2 rice cakes (4 inches across), 1 oz cheese with less than 3 g of fat, 8 large black olives, 1/2 small mango fruit, and 6 cashews.
2000	1 serving Hearty Chicken and Rice Soup, 2 rice cakes (4 inches across), 1 oz cheese with less than 3 g of fat, 8 large black olives, 1 small mango fruit, 1 cup raw nonstarchy vegetables, and 6 cashews.

This recipe courtesy of U.S.A. Rice Federation (www.usarice.com).

Hunan Turkey Salad

Serving Size: 1/6 recipe, **Total Servings:** 6

3 Tbsp creamy peanut butter
3 Tbsp soy sauce
3 Tbsp honey
1 Tbsp cider vinegar
2 tsp Chinese hot mustard
1 1/2 tsp ground ginger
1 1/2 quarts water
1 large yellow onion, cut into narrow wedges
1/2 lb peapods, trimmed
1/2 lb honey-roasted turkey breast, cut in 1/2-inch cubes
1/4 lb fresh bean sprouts
1/2 cup unsalted, dry-roasted peanuts
1-2 tsp red pepper flakes

DRESSING

1. In a small bowl, combine peanut butter, soy sauce, honey, vinegar, mustard, and ginger; set aside.

SALAD

1. In large saucepan over high heat, bring water to a boil. Add onions and peapods and boil 1 minute. Rinse and drain thoroughly.

2. In a large bowl, combine onions, peapods, turkey, bean sprouts, and peanuts. Gently fold in peanut sauce. Sprinkle with red pepper flakes.

3. Cover and refrigerate for 2–3 hours.

EXCHANGES

1 Carbohydrate	1 Very Lean Meat
1 Vegetable	2 Fat

Calories	232
Calories from Fat	98
Total Fat	11 g
Saturated Fat	2.1 g
Polyunsaturated Fat	3.3 g
Monounsaturated Fat	5.2 g
Cholesterol	15 mg
Sodium	798 mg
Total Carbohydrate	22 g
Dietary Fiber	3 g
Sugars	16 g
Protein	15 g

FITTING YOUR PLAN

Because this recipe uses a very-lean-meat exchange, you have an extra 2–3 g of fat, or 1/2 fat exchange, in this meal plan. The carbohydrate is counted as 1 starch exchange.

CALORIE PLAN

1500 (borrow 1/2 fat exchange from another meal in the day, but give 1 lean-meat exchange to another meal): 1 serving Hunan Turkey Salad, 3/4 oz pretzels, and 1 small orange.

1800 (give 1 lean-meat exchange to another part of the day): 1 serving Hunan Turkey Salad, 3/4 oz pretzels, 1 small orange, and 5 peanuts.

2000 (give 1 lean-meat exchange to another meal in the day): 1 serving Hunan Turkey Salad, 3/4 oz pretzels, 1 large orange, 5 peanuts, and 1 cup raw vegetables.

This recipe courtesy of the National Turkey Federation (www.eatturkey.com).

Idaho Potato and Kielbasa Soup

Serving Size: 1/6 recipe, **Total Servings:** 6

12 oz light or turkey kielbasa, chopped
2 lb Idaho potatoes, scrubbed and chopped
1 bay leaf
6 cups low-sodium beef or chicken broth
1 10-oz pkg frozen peas, thawed
1/2 cup minced chives, green onions, or fresh parsley (*optional*)

1. In a large stockpot, over medium-high heat, sauté kielbasa until lightly browned; remove from pot and drain on paper towels. Pour off fat and return pot to stove.

2. Add potatoes, bay leaf, and broth to the pot. Bring mixture to a boil, then reduce heat to medium and simmer for 8 minutes or until potatoes are cooked through. Remove bay leaf from pot and discard.

3. Working in batches, use a slotted spoon to lift potatoes out of broth and puree in a blender or food processor until smooth. As each is pureed, whisk each batch back into the broth.

4. Return kielbasa to the pot, add peas, and simmer 5 minutes until heated through. Ladle into bowls, garnish with chives, onions, or parsley if desired, and serve.

EXCHANGES

2 1/2 Starch   1 Lean Meat

Calories	258
Calories from Fat	47
Total Fat	5 g
Saturated Fat	2.0 g
Polyunsaturated Fat	1.1 g
Monounsaturated Fat	1.2 g
Cholesterol	32 mg
Sodium	762 mg
Total Carbohydrate	38 g
Dietary Fiber	5 g
Sugars	7 g
Protein	15 g

FITTING YOUR PLAN

CALORIE PLAN	
1500	(borrow 1/2 starch exchange from another part of the day, but save 1 lean-meat exchange for another part of the day): 1 serving Idaho Potato and Kielbasa Soup, 1/2 large fresh pear or 1 cup papaya cubes, 1 cup mixed raw vegetable sticks, and 4 English walnut halves.
1800	(borrow 1/2 starch exchange from another part of the day, but save 1 lean-meat exchange for another part of the day): 1 serving Idaho Potato and Kielbasa Soup, 1/2 large fresh pear or 1 cup papaya cubes, 1 cup mixed raw vegetable sticks, 2 Tbsp reduced-fat salad dressing, and 4 English walnut halves.
2000	(borrow 1/2 starch exchange from another part of the day, but save 1 lean-meat exchange for another part of the day): 1 serving Idaho Potato and Kielbasa Soup, 1 large fresh pear or 2 cups papaya cubes, 2 cups mixed raw vegetable sticks, 2 Tbsp reduced-fat salad dressing, and 4 English walnut halves.

This recipe courtesy of the Idaho Potato Commission (www.idahopotato.com).

Lemon Pecan Green Beans

Serving Size: 1/4 recipe, **Total Servings:** 4

1 lb fresh green beans
1/4 tsp salt, or to taste
1 Tbsp olive oil
1/4 cup green onions, sliced
1/4 cup Georgia pecans, chopped, toasted
2 tsp finely chopped fresh rosemary or 1 tsp dried rosemary
2 tsp fresh lemon juice
2 tsp grated lemon rind
Garnishes: lemon slice, fresh rosemary sprigs

1. Wash beans and remove ends. Sprinkle with salt. Arrange beans in a steamer basket and place over boiling water. Cover and steam for approximately 10 minutes or until crisp tender. Plunge green beans into cold water to stop cooking process; drain and set aside.

2. In a large skillet, heat olive oil over medium heat. Add green onions and cook, stirring constantly, about 3 minutes. Add green beans, pecans, rosemary, and lemon juice; cook, stirring constantly, until mixture is thoroughly heated. Sprinkle with lemon rind and garnish if desired. Serve immediately with grilled chicken or fish.

EXCHANGES

2 Vegetable	1 1/2 Fat

Calories 120	
Calories from Fat 83	
Total Fat . . . . 9 g	
Saturated Fat . . . . 0.9 g	
Polyunsaturated Fat . . . . 2.0 g	
Monounsaturated Fat . . . . 5.8 g	
Cholesterol . . . . 0 mg	
Sodium . . . . 150 mg	
Total Carbohydrate . . . . 9 g	
Dietary Fiber . . . . 4 g	
Sugars . . . . 2 g	
Protein . . . . 3 g	

FITTING YOUR PLAN

CALORIE PLAN

1500   1/2 serving Lemon Pecan Green Beans (save the other 1/2 serving for a snack), 2 slices whole-grain bread (1 oz each), 2 oz lean meat, 1 Tbsp fat-free mayonnaise, lettuce, 1/2 cup fruit cocktail packed in juice, and 1 pecan half.

1800   1/2 serving Lemon Pecan Green Beans (save the other 1/2 serving for a snack), 2 slices whole-grain bread (1 oz each), 2 oz lean meat, 1 Tbsp reduced-fat mayonnaise, lettuce, 1/2 cup fruit cocktail packed in juice, and 1 pecan half.

2000   1 serving Lemon Pecan Green Beans, 2 slices whole-grain bread (1 oz each), 2 oz lean meat, 1 Tbsp reduced-fat mayonnaise, lettuce, 1 cup fruit cocktail packed in juice, and 1 pecan half.

This recipe courtesy of the Georgia Pecan Commission (www.georgiapecans.org).

Northwest Chili

Serving Size: 1/8 recipe, **Total Servings:** 8

1 cup onion, chopped
2 large cloves garlic, minced
1 1/2 Tbsp canola oil
1 cup dry USA lentils, rinsed
1 cup potato, diced
1/2 cup carrots, shredded
1 green bell pepper, seeded and chopped
1 Tbsp chili powder, or to taste
2 1/2 cups water
2 tsp beef bouillon granules or 2 beef bouillon cubes
1 can (14 1/2 oz) tomatoes
1 can (8 oz) tomato sauce
1 can (15 oz) USA chickpeas, drained and rinsed, or about 2 cups boiled
1/4 tsp crushed red pepper, or to taste
Salt and freshly ground black pepper, to taste

1. In a large, heavy saucepan, cook onion and garlic in oil for 3–4 minutes. Add lentils and stir to coat them with oil.

2. Add potatoes, carrots, bell pepper, chili powder, water, and bouillon. Bring to a boil.

3. Reduce heat, cover, and simmer about 25 minutes, or until lentils are tender.

4. Add tomatoes, breaking them up as you do, and tomato sauce, chickpeas, and red pepper. Simmer for another 15 minutes. Season to taste with red pepper, salt, and black pepper.

EXCHANGES

2 Starch	1/2 Fat	1 Vegetable

Calories	198
Calories from Fat	35
Total Fat	4 g
Saturated Fat	0.3 g
Polyunsaturated Fat	1.4 g
Monounsaturated Fat	1.8 g
Cholesterol	0 mg
Sodium	564 mg
Total Carbohydrate	33 g
Dietary Fiber	10 g
Sugars	9 g
Protein	10 g

FITTING YOUR PLAN

CALORIE PLAN	
1500	(save 1/2 fat exchange for another meal): 1 serving Northwest Chili, 1 small nectarine, and 2 oz cheese with 3 g of fat or less per ounce or 4 Tbsp grated Parmesan cheese.
1800	(save 1 1/2 fat exchanges for another meal): 1 serving Northwest Chili, 1 small nectarine, and 2 oz cheese with 3 g of fat or less per ounce or 4 Tbsp grated Parmesan cheese.
2000	1 serving Northwest Chili, 1 large nectarine, 2 oz cheese with 3 g of fat or less per ounce or 4 Tbsp grated Parmesan cheese, 1 cup mixed nonstarchy vegetable salad, and 3 Tbsp reduced-fat salad dressing.

This recipe courtesy of the U.S.A. Dry Pea & Lentil Council (www.pea-lentil.com).

Pacific Shrimp Salad with Kiwifruit

Serving Size: 1/4 recipe, **Total Servings:** 4

1/2 lb California kiwifruit, pared and sliced
1/2 lb (21–30 size) shrimp, shelled, deveined, and cooked with tails intact
1/2 cup radish, finely julienned
1/2 cup pomegranate
1/2 head butter lettuce
    Lemon Ginger Dressing

1. Arrange all ingredients in a shallow, lettuce-lined salad bowl. Serve with Lemon Ginger Dressing.

Lemon Ginger Dressing

2 Tbsp oil
2 Tbsp vinegar
2 Tbsp lemon juice
1 Tbsp honey
1 tsp grated ginger
1/2 tsp salt
1/8 tsp pepper

Combine all ingredients; mix well. Makes about 1/3 cup.

EXCHANGES

1 Fruit	1 1/2 Fat
1 Very Lean Meat	

Calories	162
Calories from Fat	68
Total Fat	8 g
Saturated Fat	0.6 g
Polyunsaturated Fat	2.3 g
Monounsaturated Fat	4.1 g
Cholesterol	65 mg
Sodium	375 mg
Total Carbohydrate	17 g
Dietary Fiber	2 g
Sugars	11 g
Protein	8 g

FITTING YOUR PLAN

With the 1 very-lean-meat exchange in this recipe, the meal pattern can have an extra 0–3 g of fat, or an extra 1/2 fat exchange.

CALORIE PLAN

1500 (save 1 lean-meat exchange for another meal): 1 serving Pacific Shrimp Salad with Kiwifruit, 1 medium (2 oz) rye bread roll or medium (6 oz) baked potato, 2 Tbsp fat-free margarine spread, and 1/2 cup cooked broccoli.

1800 (save 1 lean-meat exchange for another meal): 1 serving Pacific Shrimp Salad with Kiwifruit, 1 medium (2 oz) rye bread roll or medium (6 oz) baked potato, 1 Tbsp low-fat margarine, and 1/2 cup cooked broccoli.

2000 (save 1 lean-meat exchange for another meal): 1 serving Pacific Shrimp Salad with Kiwifruit, 1 medium (2 oz) rye bread roll or medium (6 oz) baked potato, 1 Tbsp low-fat margarine, 1 cup cooked broccoli, and 12 sweet cherries.

This recipe courtesy of the California Kiwifruit Commission (www.kiwifruit.org).

Pistachio Turkey Taco Salad

Serving Size: 1/8 recipe, **Total Servings:** 8

1 small head of iceberg lettuce
8 taco shells
3 cups shredded leftover roast turkey breast or deli turkey breast (approximately 1 lb)
1 lb tomatoes, chopped (2 1/2 cups)
1 large green bell pepper, seeded and chopped (1 cup)
1/4 cup fat-free sour cream
1/3 cup natural California pistachios, chopped
Salsa Dressing

1. Shred lettuce and arrange on eight plates. Stand taco shells upright in center of each bed of lettuce; fill with turkey, tomatoes, and bell pepper. Top with sour cream and pistachios. Serve with dressing on the side.

Salsa Dressing

1 cup mild or hot bottled salsa
1 tsp lime rind, grated
2 Tbsp fresh lime juice

Mix all ingredients.

EXCHANGES

1/2 Starch	1 Very Lean Meat
2 Vegetable	1 1/2 Fat

Calories	190
Calories from Fat	70
Total Fat	8 g
Saturated Fat	1.4 g
Polyunsaturated Fat	2.5 g
Monounsaturated Fat	3.1 g
Cholesterol	27 mg
Sodium	632 mg
Total Carbohydrate	17 g
Dietary Fiber	3 g
Sugars	4 g
Protein	15 g

FITTING YOUR PLAN

Because the meal plans are based on lean-meat exchanges and this recipe uses very-lean-meat exchanges, you have an extra 0–3 g of fat (approximately 1/2 fat exchange) for this meal.

CALORIE PLAN

1500 (borrow 1 vegetable exchange from another meal and give 1 extra lean-meat exchange to another meal in the day): 1 serving Pistachio Turkey Taco Salad, 3/4 cup corn, and 1/2 cup juice-packed plums.

1800 (borrow 1 vegetable exchange from another meal and give 1 extra lean-meat exchange to another meal in the day): 1 serving Pistachio Turkey Taco Salad, 3/4 cup corn, 1/2 cup juice-packed plums, and 1 tsp margarine.

2000 (give 1 lean-meat exchange to another meal in the day): 1 serving Pistachio Turkey Taco Salad, 3/4 cup corn, 1 cup juice-packed plums, and 1 tsp margarine.

This recipe courtesy of the California Pistachio Commission (www.pistachios.org).

Potluck Pasta Salad

Serving Size: 1/12 recipe, **Total Servings:** 12

2 cups packaged dried corkscrew macaroni (rotini)
4 oz cubed reduced-fat Monterey Jack cheese
1 cup thinly sliced celery
1 cup green sweet pepper, cut into 1/2-inch pieces
1 cup sliced radishes
1/4 cup sliced green onions
3/4 cup frozen Florida orange juice concentrate, thawed
1/2 cup fat-free mayonnaise dressing
1/2 cup fat-free plain yogurt
1/4 tsp ground black pepper
4 Florida oranges, peeled, sectioned, and seeded

1. Cook pasta according to package directions. Drain. Rinse with cold water and drain again. In a large bowl, combine pasta, cheese, celery, green pepper, radishes, and green onions.

2. For dressing, in a small bowl, stir together thawed concentrate, mayonnaise, yogurt, and black pepper. Pour dressing over pasta mixture. Add orange sections. Toss gently to coat. Cover and chill for 4–24 hours.

EXCHANGES

1/2 Starch	1 Lean Meat	1 Fruit

Calories	145
Calories from Fat	19
Total Fat	2 g
Saturated Fat	1.4 g
Polyunsaturated Fat	0.2 g
Monounsaturated Fat	0.5 g
Cholesterol	7 mg
Sodium	165 mg
Total Carbohydrate	26 g
Dietary Fiber	2 g
Sugars	14 g
Protein	6 g

FITTING YOUR PLAN

CALORIE PLAN	
1500	1 serving Potluck Pasta Salad, 1 medium whole-grain dinner roll (1 1/2 oz), 1/2 cup cooked carrots, 2 sardines, and 6 almonds.
1800	1 serving Potluck Pasta Salad, 1 medium whole-grain dinner roll (1 1/2 oz), 1/2 cup cooked carrots, 2 sardines, and 12 almonds.
2000	1 serving Potluck Pasta Salad, 1 medium whole-grain dinner roll (1 1/2 oz), 17 small grapes, 1 cup cooked carrots, 2 sardines, and 12 almonds.

This recipe courtesy of the Florida Department of Citrus (www.floridajuice.com).

Practically Perfect Picnic Salad

Serving Size: 1/4 recipe, **Total Servings:** 4

1 cup California seedless grapes
1 can (15 oz) small white beans, drained
1/2 cup diced celery
1/4 cup minced green onion
2 Tbsp chopped parsley
  Lemon-Mustard Dressing
  Lettuce leaves

1. Combine all ingredients except lettuce; mix well. Serve on lettuce leaves.

Lemon-Mustard Dressing

2 Tbsp vegetable oil
2 Tbsp lemon juice
1 tsp Dijon-style mustard
1/4 tsp salt
1/4 tsp pepper

Combine all ingredients; mix well. Makes 1/4 cup.

EXCHANGES

1 1/2 Starch	1 Fat	1/2 Fruit

Calories	200
Calories from Fat	67
Total Fat	7 g
Saturated Fat	0.5 g
Polyunsaturated Fat	2.3 g
Monounsaturated Fat	4.2 g
Cholesterol	0 mg
Sodium	349 mg
Total Carbohydrate	28 g
Dietary Fiber	6 g
Sugars	8 g
Protein	7 g

FITTING YOUR PLAN

CALORIE PLAN

1500 (save 1/2 starch exchange for another meal): 1 serving Practically Perfect Picnic Salad, 6 sweet fresh cherries, 1 cup mixed raw nonstarchy vegetables, and 2 oz of cheese with 3 g of fat or less.

1800 (save 1/2 starch exchange for another meal): 1 serving Practically Perfect Picnic Salad, 1 cup mixed raw nonstarchy vegetables, 6 sweet fresh cherries, 2 oz of cheese with 3 g of fat or less, and 6 mixed nuts.

2000 (save 1/2 starch exchange for another meal): 1 serving Practically Perfect Picnic Salad, 2 cups mixed raw nonstarchy vegetables, 18 sweet fresh cherries, 2 oz of cheese with 3 g of fat or less, and 6 mixed nuts.

This recipe courtesy of the California Table Grape Commission (www.freshCaliforniagrapes.com).

Santa Fe Casserole with Cornbread Topping

Serving Size: 1/6 recipe, **Total Servings:** 6

1 lb lean ground American lamb (leg or shoulder)
1 can (15 oz) chunky tomato sauce with salsa
1 can (15 oz) black or pinto beans, drained and rinsed
1 pkg (6 1/2 oz) corn muffin mix

1. In a saucepan, cook ground lamb until brown, stirring frequently to break up chunks. Drain well. Stir in tomato sauce and drained beans. Pour into 8 X 8 X 2-inch baking dish.

2. Prepare corn muffin mix according to package directions using nonfat milk. Pour evenly over meat mixture. Bake in preheated 400°F oven for 20–25 minutes or until cornbread is done. Cut in squares and serve.

EXCHANGES

2 Starch	2 Lean Meat	1 Vegetable

Calories	303
Calories from Fat	70
Total Fat	8 g
Saturated Fat	2.3 g
Polyunsaturated Fat	0.8 g
Monounsaturated Fat	3.2 g
Cholesterol	49 mg
Sodium	797 mg
Total Carbohydrate	37 g
Dietary Fiber	5 g
Sugars	7 g
Protein	22 g

FITTING YOUR PLAN

CALORIE PLAN	
1500	1 serving Santa Fe Casserole with Cornbread Topping, 1 small orange, and 6 mixed nuts.
1800	1 serving Santa Fe Casserole with Cornbread Topping, 1 small orange, and 12 mixed nuts.
2000	1 serving Santa Fe Casserole with Cornbread Topping, 1 large orange, 1/2 cup Brussels sprouts, and 12 mixed nuts.

This recipe courtesy of the American Lamb Board (www.americanlambboard.org).

Santa Rosa Shrimp

Serving Size: 1/6 recipe, **Total Servings:** 6

1 1/2 lb raw, peeled, and deveined
Florida shrimp
2 Tbsp minced Florida garlic
1 Tbsp Florida lime juice
1 tsp ground thyme
1 tsp salt
1/2 tsp white pepper
Nonstick cooking spray
2 cups fresh Florida corn kernels
1 cup chopped Florida green
bell peppers
1 cup chopped Florida red bell
peppers
1/2 cup chopped Florida onions
1 large Florida tomato, cut in
8 pieces

1. Drain shrimp of all excess water. In
a large mixing bowl, combine shrimp,
garlic, lime juice, thyme, salt, and white
pepper; mix until well coated.
2. Lightly oil a large skillet with
cooking spray and cook shrimp on

medium high for 6–8 minutes, stirring occasionally. Remove shrimp
from skillet; set aside.

3. In the same skillet, add corn, bell
peppers, and onion; cook on medium
heat until corn is tender. Add shrimp
and tomatoes to skillet and cook until
shrimp are opaque in the center.

EXCHANGES

1/2 Starch	3 Very Lean Meat	1 Vegetable

Calories	155
Calories from Fat	16
Total Fat	2 g
Saturated Fat	0.4 g
Polyunsaturated Fat	0.8 g
Monounsaturated Fat	0.4 g
Cholesterol	162 mg
Sodium	587 mg
Total Carbohydrate	16 g
Dietary Fiber	3 g
Sugars	6 g
Protein	20 g

FITTING YOUR PLAN

Because this recipe has 3 very-lean-meat exchanges, you can have an extra 6–9 g of fat for the meal, or about an extra 1 1/2 fat exchange. These are included in the nuts found in the plans below.

CALORIE PLAN

1500   (for the day, save your breakfast meat exchange and add it to lunch): 1 serving Santa Rosa Shrimp, 1/2 cup rice, 1 tsp margarine, 3/4 cup mixed mandarin oranges and blueberries, and 6 pecan halves.

1800   (for the day, save your breakfast meat exchange and add it to lunch): 1 serving Santa Rosa Shrimp, 1/2 cup rice, 2 tsp margarine, 3/4 cup mixed mandarin oranges and blueberries, and 6 pecan halves.

2000   (for the day, save your breakfast meat exchange and add it to lunch): 1 serving Santa Rosa Shrimp, 1/2 cup rice, 2 tsp margarine, 1 1/2 cups mixed mandarin oranges and blueberries, 1/2 cup Italian beans, and 6 pecan halves.

This recipe courtesy of the Florida Department of Agriculture (www.florida-agriculture.com).

Sliced Tomatoes with Blue Cheese and Pine Nuts

Serving Size: 1/6 recipe, **Total Servings:** 6

3 large (about 1 1/2 lb) fresh
California tomatoes, sliced
1 tsp finely chopped garlic
2 Tbsp olive oil
Sprinkle of pepper
2 Tbsp toasted pine nuts
1/2 oz blue cheese
1/2 Tbsp chopped parsley

1. Slice California tomatoes and arrange, overlapping, on a platter. Mix garlic with oil and drizzle over California tomatoes. Sprinkle with pepper and pine nuts and top with crumbled cheese and parsley. Let sit at room temperature 15 minutes before serving.

EXCHANGES

1 Vegetable	1 1/2 Fat

Calories	86
Calories from Fat	65
Total Fat	7 g
Saturated Fat	1.4 g
Polyunsaturated Fat	1.2 g
Monounsaturated Fat	4.2 g
Cholesterol	2 mg
Sodium	42 mg
Total Carbohydrate	5 g
Dietary Fiber	1 g
Sugars	3 g
Protein	2 g

FITTING YOUR PLAN

CALORIE PLAN	
1500	(borrow 1/2 fat exchange from snack): 1 serving Sliced Tomatoes with Blue Cheese and Pine Nuts, 1 small (1 oz) whole-grain roll, 1/2 large corncob, 1 1/4 cups watermelon, and 2 oz salmon.
1800	1 serving Sliced Tomatoes with Blue Cheese and Pine Nuts, 1 small (1 oz) whole-grain roll, 1/2 large corncob, 1 1/4 cups watermelon, 2 oz salmon, and 1 1/2 tsp reduced-fat margarine.
2000	1 serving Sliced Tomatoes with Blue Cheese and Pine Nuts, 1 small (1 oz) whole-grain roll, 1/2 large corncob, 1/2 cup cooked green beans, 2 1/2 cups watermelon, 2 oz salmon, and 1 1/2 tsp reduced-fat margarine.

This recipe courtesy of the California Tomato Commission (www.tomato.org).

Slim Strawberry Chef's Salad

Serving Size: 1/4 recipe, **Total Servings:** 4

2/3 cup nonfat light sour cream substitute

1/4 cup red wine vinegar

2 green onions, sliced

2–3 tsp hot-sweet mustard
Salt and pepper, to taste
Butter lettuce leaves

2 pint baskets California strawberries, stemmed

2 cups assorted fresh fruit pieces (1/2 cup each of grapefruit segments, pineapple chunks, and orange and kiwi slices)

7 slices (1 oz each) lean turkey and/or ham

1. To make salad dressing, in a small bowl, whisk sour cream substitute, vinegar, onions, and mustard; season with salt and pepper. Set aside.

2. To assemble salad, line four dinner plates with lettuce. Top with fruits and turkey, dividing equally. Serve with dressing on the side.

EXCHANGES

2 Fruit	1/2 Fat	2 Very Lean Meat

Calories	215
Calories from Fat	31
Total Fat	3 g
Saturated Fat	0.5 g
Polyunsaturated Fat	1.1 g
Monounsaturated Fat	0.7 g
Cholesterol	37 mg
Sodium	300 mg
Total Carbohydrate	32 g
Dietary Fiber	6 g
Sugars	20 g
Protein	16 g

FITTING YOUR PLAN

These meals are calculated with very-lean-meat exchanges, which contain 0–1 g of fat per ounce. Lean meat contains 3 g of fat per ounce. Therefore, 4–6 g of fat (about 5 g) or 1 fat exchange will be added to this meal because there are 2 very-lean-meat exchanges calculated in the recipe. In the meal plan below, the 1/2 cup of sugar-free pudding counts as 1 starch exchange and the 2-inch cube of corn bread counts as 1 starch and 1 fat exchange.

CALORIE PLAN

1500 (borrow 1 fruit exchange from breakfast): 1 serving Slim Strawberry Chef's Salad, 1/2 cup cooked Brussels sprouts, 2-inch cube of corn bread, 1/2 cup sugar-free pudding cup, and 1 1/2 tsp low-fat margarine.

1800 (borrow 1 fruit exchange from breakfast): 1 serving Slim Strawberry Chef's Salad, 1/2 cup cooked Brussels sprouts, 2-inch cube of corn bread, 1 1/2 tsp margarine, and 1/2 cup sugar-free pudding cup.

2000 1 serving Slim Strawberry Chef's Salad, 2-inch cube of corn bread, 1 cup cooked Brussels sprouts, 1 1/2 tsp margarine, and 1/2 cup sugar-free pudding cup.

This recipe courtesy of the California Strawberry Commission (www.calstrawberry.com).

Springtime Stir-Fry with Scallops and California Jumbo Asparagus

Serving Size: 1/4 recipe, **Total Servings:** 4

3/4 lb fresh California asparagus
3/4 cup reduced-sodium chicken broth
1 Tbsp cornstarch
1 tsp light soy sauce
3/4 lb sea scallops
1 cup sliced button mushrooms or 3–4 oyster mushrooms
1 tsp sesame oil
1 medium clove garlic
1 cup cherry tomato halves
2–3 thin green onions
2 cups hot cooked rice (no salt added)

1. Trim or break off asparagus spears at tender point; rinse and cut into 2-inch diagonal pieces. Cook asparagus until crisp tender, about 3–5 minutes. Do not overcook. Drain and rinse under cold water.

2. Combine chicken broth, cornstarch, and soy sauce and set aside.

3. Stir-fry halved scallops and mushrooms in oil with garlic until scallops are just cooked through, about 4 minutes.

4. Stir in cornstarch mixture. Cook, stirring, until sauce thickens. Add drained asparagus, tomatoes, and green onions; heat. Add pepper to taste. Serve over rice.

EXCHANGES

1 1/2 Starch	2 Very Lean Meat
1 Vegetable	

Calories 219
   Calories from Fat 23
Total Fat . . . . 3 g
   Saturated Fat . . . . 0.3 g
   Polyunsaturated Fat. . . . . 1.0 g
   Monounsaturated Fat . . . . 0.6 g
Cholesterol . . . . 34 mg
Sodium. . . . . 320 mg
Total Carbohydrate . . . . 29 g
   Dietary Fiber. . . . . 2 g
   Sugars . . . . 3 g
Protein . . . . 19 g

FITTING YOUR PLAN

The calculations for the meal plans are based on lean-meat exchanges. This recipe has very-lean-meat exchanges; therefore, you can have an extra 4–6 g of fat (about 1 fat exchange) in the meal.

CALORIE PLAN

1500   (save 1/2 starch exchange for another meal): 1 serving Springtime Stir-Fry with Scallops and California Jumbo Asparagus, 1/2 cup canned plums in extra-light syrup, and 20 peanuts.

1800   (save 1/2 starch exchange and 1 fat exchange for another meal): 1 serving Springtime Stir-Fry with Scallops and California Jumbo Asparagus, 1/2 cup canned plums in extra-light syrup, and 20 peanuts.

2000   (save 1/2 starch exchange and 1 fat exchange for another meal): 1 serving Springtime Stir-Fry with Scallops and California Jumbo Asparagus, 1 cup canned plums in extra-light syrup, 1/2 cup zucchini and tomatoes, and 20 peanuts.

This recipe courtesy of the California Asparagus Commission (www.calasparagus.com).

Stewed Fresh Sweet Corn with Tomatoes

Serving Size: 1/4 recipe, **Total Servings:** 4

2 cans (14 1/2 oz each) Italian stewed tomatoes
4 medium ears fresh sweet corn, husked and cut in 2-inch pieces
4 slices (1/2 inch thick, about 3/4 oz each) toasted Italian bread
1/4 cup freshly grated Parmesan cheese
Garnish: parsley, chopped (*optional*)

1. Place tomatoes in a large skillet; break up the larger pieces with a spoon. Cover and bring to a simmer; add sweet corn; cover and simmer until corn is tender, about 5 minutes, turning corn halfway through cooking. To serve, place a slice of bread in the bottom of an individual bowl, spoon in tomatoes and top with sweet corn, and sprinkle with the cheese. Garnish with chopped parsley, if desired.

EXCHANGES
2 Starch   1/2 Fat   2 Vegetable

Calories	220
Calories from Fat	31
Total Fat	3 g
Saturated Fat	1.3 g
Polyunsaturated Fat	0.8 g
Monounsaturated Fat	1.0 g
Cholesterol	5 mg
Sodium	619 mg
Total Carbohydrate	42 g
Dietary Fiber	6 g
Sugars	12 g
Protein	9 g

FITTING YOUR PLAN

CALORIE PLAN	
1500	(borrow 1 vegetable exchange from a snack): 1 serving Stewed Fresh Sweet Corn with Tomatoes, 1 small (4 oz) banana, 2 oz lean baked chicken or fish, and 3 cashews.
1800	(borrow 1 vegetable exchange from a snack): 1 serving Stewed Fresh Sweet Corn with Tomatoes, 1 small (4 oz) banana, 2 oz lean baked chicken or fish, and 9 cashews.
2000	1 serving Stewed Fresh Sweet Corn with Tomatoes, 1 large (8 oz) banana, 2 oz lean baked chicken or fish, and 9 cashews.

This recipe courtesy of the Fresh Super Sweet Corn Council (www.freshsupersweetcorn.com).

Sweet Potato and Kale Soup

Serving Size: 1/8 recipe, **Total Servings:** 8

5 cups low-sodium chicken broth, defatted and divided
1 1/2 cups onion, chopped
3 cups fresh kale, chopped
3 cups peeled sweet potato, diced
1 cup smoked turkey breast, diced
Seasonings, to taste
8 slices low-fat Wisconsin Muenster cheese (3/4 oz per slice)

1. In a stock pot, heat 1/2 cup broth and onion. Simmer, covered, 5 minutes. Add kale, sweet potatoes, turkey, and remaining 4 1/2 cups chicken broth; return to a simmer and cook 35–40 minutes or until kale and potatoes are tender. Adjust seasoning, if desired. To serve, ladle 1 cup soup into crock and top with a slice of Muenster. Serve hot.

EXCHANGES

1 Starch	1 Lean Meat
1 Vegetable	1/2 Fat

Calories	173
Calories from Fat	48
Total Fat	5 g
Saturated Fat	2.7 g
Polyunsaturated Fat	0.6 g
Monounsaturated Fat	1.4 g
Cholesterol	22 mg
Sodium	382 mg
Total Carbohydrate	19 g
Dietary Fiber	2 g
Sugars	6 g
Protein	13 g

FITTING YOUR PLAN

CALORIE PLAN	
1500	1 serving Sweet Potato and Kale Soup, 1 small apple, and 1/2 grilled cheese sandwich made from the following ingredients: 1 slice whole-wheat bread (1 oz), 1 oz low-fat Wisconsin cheese (with less than 3 g of fat), and 1 1/2 tsp low-fat margarine.
1800	1 serving Sweet Potato and Kale Soup, 1 small apple, 3 mixed nuts, and 1/2 grilled cheese sandwich made from the following ingredients: 1 slice whole-wheat bread (1 oz), 1 oz low-fat Wisconsin cheese (with less than 3 g of fat), and 1 tsp margarine.
2000	1 serving Sweet Potato and Kale Soup, 1 large apple (8 oz), 3 mixed nuts, 1 cup raw vegetables, and 1/2 grilled cheese sandwich made from the following ingredients: 1 slice whole-wheat bread (1 oz), 1 oz low-fat Wisconsin cheese (with less than 3 g of fat), and 1 tsp margarine.

This recipe courtesy of the Wisconsin Milk Marketing Board (www.wisdairy.com).

Sweet Potato Black Bean Salad

Serving Size: 1/8 recipe, **Total Servings:** 8

1 lb cooked cubed sweet potatoes
1 1/2 cups black beans (cooked)
1 cup julienned roasted peppers (combine red, yellow, and green)
1 medium ripe papaya, peeled and sliced
3/4 cup watercress
1/2 cup chopped purple onion
1/2 tsp chili powder
3 Tbsp garlic–flavored olive oil
2 Tbsp red wine vinegar
1/4 tsp hot pepper sauce

1. In large bowl, combine all ingredients. Toss to blend. Cover and let stand at room temperature for 15 minutes or refrigerate for 1 hour. To serve, spoon onto fresh greens and garnish with crisp fried tortilla strips.

EXCHANGES

1 1/2 Starch	1 Fat

Calories 154	
Calories from Fat 49	
Total Fat . . . . 5 g	
Saturated Fat . . . . 0.8 g	
Polyunsaturated Fat . . . . 0.6 g	
Monounsaturated Fat . . . . 3.8 g	
Cholesterol . . . . 0 mg	
Sodium. . . . . 22 mg	
Total Carbohydrate . . . . 23 g	
Dietary Fiber. . . . . 6 g	
Sugars . . . . 8 g	
Protein . . . . 4 g	

FITTING YOUR PLAN

CALORIE PLAN	
1500	1 serving Sweet Potato Black Bean Salad, 12 oyster crackers, 2 oz lean meat, 4 fresh apricots, and 1 cup mixed raw nonstarchy vegetables.
1800	1 serving Sweet Potato Black Bean Salad, 12 oyster crackers, 2 oz lean meat, 4 fresh apricots, 1 cup mixed raw nonstarchy vegetables, and 2 Tbsp reduced-fat salad dressing.
2000	1 serving Sweet Potato Black Bean Salad, 12 oyster crackers, 2 oz lean meat, 4 fresh apricots, 1 kiwi, 2 cups mixed raw nonstarchy vegetables, and 2 Tbsp reduced-fat salad dressing.

This recipe courtesy of the North Carolina Sweetpotato Commission (www.ncsweetpotatoes.com).

The MLT

Serving Size: 1 sandwich, **Total Servings:** 4

Nonstick cooking spray
8 oz white mushroom or mixed
mushrooms (such as white
mushrooms and shiitake), sliced
(about 3 cups)
1/2 tsp salt
1/2 tsp ground black pepper
8 slices whole-wheat bread, toasted
1/4 cup light mayonnaise
4 lettuce leaves
4 tomato slices
2 Tbsp cooked crumbled bacon
(or jarred bacon bits)

1. Coat a large skillet with nonstick cooking spray, heat over medium heat. Add mushrooms; cook and stir until tender, about 10 minutes. Season with salt and pepper. Spread one side of each toast slice with mayonnaise. Top four slices with lettuce, tomato, and the mushroom mixture; sprinkle bacon bits on top, dividing evenly. Top with the remaining slices of toast.

EXCHANGES

2 Starch	1 1/2 Fat

Calories 227	
Calories from Fat 85	
Total Fat . . . . 9 g	
Saturated Fat . . . . 2.0 g	
Polyunsaturated Fat . . . . 2.9 g	
Monounsaturated Fat . . . . 3.2 g	
Cholesterol . . . . 8 mg	
Sodium. . . . . 766 mg	
Total Carbohydrate . . . . 31 g	
Dietary Fiber. 5 g	
Sugars . . . . 4 g	
Protein . . . . 8 g	

FITTING YOUR PLAN

CALORIE PLAN

1500 (borrow 1/2 fat exchange from another meal in the day): 1 serving MLT sandwich (move 2 lean-meat exchanges to other meals or have 1/2 cup of 4.5% fat cottage cheese with the sandwich), 1/2 cup cooked broccoli and mushrooms, and 3/4 cup blackberry and melon fruit salad.

1800 1 serving MLT sandwich (move 2 lean-meat exchanges to other meals or have 1/2 cup of 4.5% fat cottage cheese with the sandwich), 1/2 cup cooked broccoli and mushrooms, 3/4 cup blackberry and melon fruit salad, and 6 mixed nuts.

2000 1 serving MLT sandwich (move 2 lean-meat exchanges to other meals or have 1/2 cup 4.5% fat cottage cheese with the sandwich), 1 1/2 cups blackberry and melon fruit salad, 1 cup cooked broccoli and mushrooms, and 6 mixed nuts.

This recipe courtesy of the Mushroom Information Center (www.mushroominfo.com).

Tuna Apple Tortilla Wraps

Serving Size: 1 sandwich, **Total Servings:** 2

2 tortillas (8 inches each)
2 Tbsp spread (such as fat-free herbed cream cheese, pureed roasted peppers, hummus, or baba ghanoush)
1 large sweet-tart apple, washed, cored, and thinly sliced
1 can (6 1/2 oz) tuna in water, drained
1/2 to 1 Tbsp reduced-fat mayonnaise or sour cream
Freshly ground pepper, to taste
Mild curry powder (*optional*)
2 scallions with green tops, cut in half, then sliced lengthwise

1. Place the tortillas on dinner plates and spread each with 1 Tbsp of the spread. Arrange apple slices down the center of the tortillas, staying well within 1 inch from the edges.

2. In a small bowl, flake the tuna and combine with the mayonnaise and pepper. Spoon the tuna mixture over the apple slices. Sprinkle with a dash of mild curry powder, if desired. Top with the scallions. Roll the wraps from front to back and serve immediately.

EXCHANGES

2 Starch	3 Very Lean Meat
1 Fruit	1/2 Fat

Calories 333
    Calories from Fat 48
Total Fat . . . . 5 g
    Saturated Fat . . . . 1.2 g
    Polyunsaturated Fat. . . . . 1.3 g
    Monounsaturated Fat . . . . 2.3 g
Cholesterol . . . . 28 mg
Sodium. . . . . 622 mg
Total Carbohydrate . . . . 43 g
    Dietary Fiber. 4 g
    Sugars . . . . 13 g
Protein . . . . 28 g

FITTING YOUR PLAN

The meal patterns are calculated for lean-meat exchanges. Because the exchanges in this recipe are very-lean-meat exchanges, which have 0–1 g of fat per ounce, and lean meat has 3 g of fat per ounce, you may have an extra 6–9 g of fat (approximately 1 1/2 exchanges) in this calculation.

CALORIE PLAN

1500   (borrow 1 lean-meat exchange from breakfast): 1 serving Tuna Apple Tortilla Wraps, 1 cup raw nonstarchy vegetable sticks, and 8 walnut halves.

1800   (borrow 1 lean-meat exchange from breakfast): 1 serving Tuna Apple Tortilla Wraps, 1 cup raw nonstarchy vegetable sticks, 8 walnut halves, and 1 Tbsp salad dressing.

2000   (borrow 1 lean-meat exchange from breakfast): 1 serving Tuna Apple Tortilla Wraps, 1 small apple, 2 cups raw nonstarchy vegetable sticks, 8 walnut halves, and 1 Tbsp salad dressing.

This recipe courtesy of the U.S. Apple Association (www.usapple.org).

Vegetable Frittata

Serving Size: 1/4 recipe, **Total Servings:** 4

Nonstick cooking spray
1 1/2 cups chopped broccoli or 1 pkg (10 oz) frozen chopped broccoli
1/2 cup diced carrot (about 1 medium)
1/4 cup water
3 whole eggs and 10 egg whites
3/4 cup (3 oz) shredded low-fat Cheddar cheese
1/2 cup nonfat milk
1 Tbsp instant minced onion
2 tsp prepared mustard
1/8 tsp pepper

1. Evenly coat a 10-inch omelet pan or skillet with ovenproof handle with spray (to make a handle ovenproof, wrap it completely with aluminum foil). Add broccoli, carrot, and water. Cover and cook over medium-high heat until carrot is crisp tender, about 5–10 minutes. (Uncover and stir occasionally, if necessary, to break apart frozen broccoli.) Drain well. Return vegetables to pan. Set aside.

2. In a large bowl, beat together eggs, cheese, milk, onion, mustard, and pep-per until well blended. Pour over reserved vegetables. Cover and cook over medium heat until eggs are almost set, about 8–10 minutes. Uncover and broil about 6 inches from heat until eggs are completely set in center, about 2–3 minutes, or let stand, covered, until eggs are completely set in center, about 8–10 minutes. Cut into wedges and serve from pan, slide from pan, or invert onto serving platter.

EXCHANGES

2 Vegetable	1/2 Fat	3 Very Lean Meat

Calories	178
Calories from Fat	54
Total Fat	6 g
Saturated Fat	2.3 g
Polyunsaturated Fat	0.7 g
Monounsaturated Fat	1.9 g
Cholesterol	166 mg
Sodium	401 mg
Total Carbohydrate	8 g
Dietary Fiber	3 g
Sugars	5 g
Protein	23 g

FITTING YOUR PLAN

Because these meal plans are based on lean-meat exchanges, you have an extra 6–9 g of fat (approximately 1 1/2 fat exchanges) in this meal.

CALORIE PLAN

1500 (borrow 1 lean-meat exchange from breakfast and 1 vegetable exchange from dinner): 1 serving Vegetable Frittata, 2 slices (1 oz each) pumpernickel toast, 1 1/4 cups watermelon, 6 mixed nuts, and 1 Tbsp low-fat margarine.

1800 (borrow 1 lean-meat exchange from breakfast and 1 vegetable exchange from dinner): 1 serving Vegetable Frittata, 2 slices (1 oz each) pumpernickel toast, 1 1/4 cups watermelon, 6 mixed nuts, and 2 Tbsp low-fat margarine.

2000 (borrow 1 lean-meat exchange from breakfast): 1 serving Vegetable Frittata, 2 slices (1 oz each) pumpernickel toast, 2 1/2 cups watermelon, 6 mixed nuts, and 2 Tbsp low-fat margarine.

Dinner

Apple Chicken Stir-Fry

Serving Size: 1/4 recipe, **Total Servings:** 4

1 lb cubed boneless, skinless chicken breast

1 1/2 Tbsp canola oil

1/2 cup onion, vertically sliced

1 cup (2 medium) carrots, thinly sliced

1 tsp dried basil, crushed

1 cup fresh or frozen Chinese pea pods

1 Tbsp water

1 medium apple, cored and thinly sliced

2 cups cooked rice

1. Stir-fry cubed chicken breast in 1 Tbsp canola oil in a nonstick skillet until lightly browned and cooked. Remove from skillet.

2. Stir-fry onion, carrots, and basil in oil in the same skillet until carrots are tender.

3. Stir in pea pods and water; stir-fry for 2 minutes. Remove from heat; stir in apple. Add to chicken, serve hot over cooked rice.

EXCHANGES

1 1/2 Starch	3 Very Lean Meat
1/2 Fruit	1 Fat
1 Vegetable	

Calories	336
Calories from Fat	76
Total Fat	8 g
Saturated Fat	1.2 g
Polyunsaturated Fat	2.3 g
Monounsaturated Fat	4.1 g
Cholesterol	69 mg
Sodium	83 mg
Total Carbohydrate	36 g
Dietary Fiber	3 g
Sugars	9 g
Protein	28 g

FITTING YOUR PLAN

Because this recipe has 3 very-lean-meat exchanges, an extra 6–9 g of fat (approximately 1 1/2 fat exchanges) may be added.

CALORIE PLAN

1500   (borrow 1 meat exchange from breakfast, but give an extra 1/2 starch exchange to another meal in your day): 1 serving Chicken Apple Stir-Fry, 8 oz nonfat milk, 1/2 cup red beets, 10 walnut halves, and 1 Tbsp raisins.

1800   (give an extra 1/2 starch exchange to another meal in your day): 1 serving Chicken Apple Stir-Fry, 8 oz nonfat milk, 1/2 cup red beets, 10 walnut halves, and 1 Tbsp raisins.

2000   (give an extra 1/2 starch exchange to another meal in your day): 1 serving Chicken Apple Stir-Fry, 8 oz nonfat milk, 1/2 cup red beets, 10 walnut halves, and 1 Tbsp raisins.

This recipe courtesy of the U.S. Apple Association (www.usapple.org).

Asian-Style Fruit Slaw

Serving Size: 1/8 recipe, **Total Servings:** 8

FOR THE DRESSING
1/4 cup canola oil
1/4 cup seasoned rice vinegar
1 Tbsp fresh ginger, finely minced
1 Tbsp soy sauce

FOR THE SLAW
1 medium head Napa cabbage (also called Chinese cabbage), sliced thin
1 cup red cabbage, sliced thin
3 California plums or 2 California peaches or nectarines, rinsed and sliced into thin wedges
1/2 cup green onions, sliced diagonally
1/2 cup cashews, roughly chopped or broken
1/3 cup cilantro, chopped
1/4 cup candied ginger, slivered fine

1. Assemble the dressing by placing all ingredients in a small bowl; whisk to combine. For the slaw, place all ingredients in a large bowl and toss with dressing to combine.

EXCHANGES

1/2 Carbohydrate	2 1/2 Fat	1 Vegetable

Calories	159
Calories from Fat	100
Total Fat	11 g
Saturated Fat	1.4 g
Polyunsaturated Fat	2.8 g
Monounsaturated Fat	6.5 g
Cholesterol	0 mg
Sodium	193 mg
Total Carbohydrate	15 g
Dietary Fiber	2 g
Sugars	9 g
Protein	3 g

FITTING YOUR PLAN

For this recipe, the carbohydrate content is considered 1/2 fruit exchange.

CALORIE PLAN

1500 (borrow 1/2 fat exchange from another meal): 1 serving Asian-Style Fruit Slaw, 8 oz nonfat milk, 2/3 cup rice, 1/2 cup cooked carrots, 1 small plum, and 2 oz lean chicken, fish, beef, or pork.

1800 (borrow 1/2 fat exchange from another meal): 1 serving Asian-Style Fruit Slaw, 8 oz nonfat milk, 2/3 cup rice, 1/2 cup cooked carrots, 1 small plum, and 3 oz lean chicken, fish, beef, or pork.

2000 (borrow 1/2 fat exchange from another meal): 1 serving Asian-Style Fruit Slaw, 8 oz nonfat milk, 2/3 cup rice, 1/2 cup cooked carrots, 1 small plum, and 3 oz lean chicken, fish, beef, or pork.

This recipe courtesy of the California Tree Fruit Agreement (www.eatcaliforniafruit.com).

Asparagus and Citrus Salad

Serving Size: 1/4 recipe, **Total Servings:** 4

2 Tbsp shallots, finely chopped
1 Tbsp balsamic vinegar
1 Tbsp sherry vinegar or dry sherry
4 medium oranges (preferably blood oranges)
2–3 Tbsp extra-virgin olive oil
1/4 tsp salt and freshly ground pepper to taste
1 1/2 lb fresh California asparagus, trimmed
4 Tbsp coarsely chopped, toasted walnuts

1. In a small bowl, combine shallots with the vinegar and sherry; let stand at least 20 minutes. Meanwhile, zest one of the oranges, avoiding the white pith. Finely chop the zest and add to the shallots. Squeeze 1/3 cup juice from zested orange and add to the bowl. Slowly whisk in the olive oil and season with salt and pepper; set aside.

2. Cut asparagus spears in half or in fourths and cook in boiling salted water for 4–5 minutes until crisp tender; drain well and remove from pan to cool. Toss the vinaigrette with the cooled asparagus. Cut the ends of the remaining oranges and peel them by cutting down the fruit vertically, following the contours of the fruit.

3. Slice the peeled orange horizontally into 1/2-inch thick slices. Arrange the orange slices and asparagus spears on salad plates and season to taste with additional salt and pepper. Top each serving with 1 Tbsp toasted walnuts.

EXCHANGES

1 Fruit	2 Fat	2 Vegetable

Calories	207
Calories from Fat	109
Total Fat	12 g
Saturated Fat	1.4 g
Polyunsaturated Fat	4.2 g
Monounsaturated Fat	5.7 g
Cholesterol	0 mg
Sodium	155 mg
Total Carbohydrate	24 g
Dietary Fiber	6 g
Sugars	17 g
Protein	5 g

FITTING YOUR PLAN

CALORIE PLAN	
1500	1 serving Asparagus and Citrus Salad, 2/3 cup rice, 1 cup nonfat milk, and 2 oz grilled salmon.
1800	1 serving Asparagus and Citrus Salad, 2/3 cup rice, 1 cup nonfat milk, and 3 oz grilled salmon.
2000	1 serving Asparagus and Citrus Salad, 2/3 cup rice, 1 cup nonfat milk, and 3 oz grilled salmon.

This recipe courtesy of the California Asparagus Commission (www.calasparagus.com).

**Burgundy Beef and
Vegetable Stew, p. 93**
*Photo courtesy of the Cattlemen's Beef Board,
Texas Beef Council, National Cattlemen's Beef Association.*

(clockwise from top left)

French Toast with Poached Plums, p. 35
Photo courtesy of the California Tree Fruit Agreement.

Watermelon Blueberry Banana Split, p. 44
Photo courtesy of the National Watermelon Promotion Board.

Carmelized Salmon with Cherry Salsa, p. 95
Photo courtesy of the Cherry Marketing Institute
(www.usacherries.com).

Almond-Chicken Pear Salad, p. 48
Photo courtesy of the Pear Bureau Northwest.

(clockwise from top left)

Technicolor Vegetable Sauté, p. 131
Photo courtesy of the California Olive Industry.

Hearty Chicken and Rice Soup, p. 65
Photo courtesy of the U.S.A. Rice Federation.

California Guacamole, p. 53
Photo courtesy of the California Avocado Commission.

Black Bean and Lentil Supper

Serving Size: 1/6 recipe, **Total Servings:** 6

Nonstick cooking spray
2 cups carrots, sliced
2 cups fresh mushrooms, sliced
1/2 cup onion, chopped
2 cups Florida orange juice
1/2 tsp garlic salt
1 cup dry lentils, rinsed and drained
1 can (15 oz) black beans, rinsed and drained
2 cups frozen whole-kernel corn
1 cup shredded reduced-fat cheddar cheese (4 oz)

1. Spray an unheated large saucepan with nonstick cooking spray. Add carrots, mushrooms, and onion; cook over medium heat until tender. Carefully stir in orange juice and garlic salt. Bring to boiling. Add lentils. Return to boiling; reduce heat.

Simmer, covered, for 50 minutes. Add black beans and corn. Cook 5–10 minutes more or until lentils are tender and liquid is almost absorbed. Stir in 1/2 cup of the cheese. To serve, sprinkle each serving with some of the remaining cheese.

EXCHANGES

2 1/2 Starch	1 Vegetable
1/2 Fruit	1 Lean Meat

Calories	311
Calories from Fat	46
Total Fat	5 g
Saturated Fat	2.5 g
Polyunsaturated Fat	0.6 g
Monounsaturated Fat	1.3 g
Cholesterol	13 mg
Sodium	352 mg
Total Carbohydrate	52 g
Dietary Fiber	13 g
Sugars	15 g
Protein	19 g

FITTING YOUR PLAN

CALORIE PLAN

1500 (borrow 1/2 starch exchange from snack and add 1 meat exchange to another meal): 1 serving Black Bean and Lentil Supper, 1 small tangerine, 1/2 cup Brussels sprouts, 8 oz nonfat milk, and 12 mixed nuts.

1800 (borrow 1/2 starch exchange from snack and add 2 meat exchanges to another meal): 1 serving Black Bean and Lentil Supper, 1 small tangerine, 1/2 cup Brussels sprouts, 8 oz nonfat milk, and 12 mixed nuts.

2000 (borrow 1/2 starch exchange from snack and add 2 meat exchanges to another meal): 1 serving Black Bean and Lentil Supper, 1 small tangerine, 1/2 cup Brussels sprouts, 8 oz nonfat milk, and 12 mixed nuts.

This recipe courtesy of the Florida Department of Agriculture (www.florida-agriculture.com).

Broiled Flounder Continental

Serving Size: 1/6 recipe, **Total Servings:** 6

1 1/2 lb fish fillets (flounder, sole, or cod)
1/4 tsp salt
1/4 tsp ground black pepper
2 Tbsp cornstarch
1/2 tsp garlic powder
1/4 tsp dill weed
1 1/2 cups fat-free, reduced-sodium chicken broth
1 can (4 oz) sliced mushrooms, drained
1/2 cup peeled and deveined cooked shrimp, sliced in half lengthwise
1/2 large cucumber, sliced paper thin
1/2 cup chopped onion
1 Tbsp corn-oil margarine
3 cups cooked rice
2 Tbsp chopped pimientos

1. Arrange fillets in a greased shallow baking dish; sprinkle with salt and pepper. Broil 10 minutes.

2. Combine cornstarch, garlic, dill weed, and broth in a medium saucepan. Cook over low heat, stirring constantly, until thickened. Stir in mushrooms and shrimp. Pour over fillets and broil 5 minutes longer.

3. Cook cucumber and onion in margarine in a large skillet until tender crisp. Add rice and pimientos; heat thoroughly. Serve with broiled fish.

EXCHANGES

1 1/2 Starch	3 Very Lean Meat
1 Vegetable	

Calories 262	
Calories from Fat 29	
Total Fat . . . . 3 g	
Saturated Fat . . . . 0.7 g	
Polyunsaturated Fat. . . . . 1.4 g	
Monounsaturated Fat . . . . 0.7 g	
Cholesterol . . . . 80 mg	
Sodium. . . . . 412 mg	
Total Carbohydrate . . . . 29 g	
Dietary Fiber. . . . . 2 g	
Sugars . . . . 2 g	
Protein . . . . 28 g	

FITTING YOUR PLAN

With this recipe, you get an extra 6–9 g of fat in the meal plan (approximately 1 1/2 extra fat exchanges) because it has very-lean-meat exchanges rather than lean-meat exchanges.

CALORIE PLAN

1500 (borrow 1 meat exchange from another meal, but add 1 1/2 fat exchanges to another meal): 1 serving Broiled Flounder Continental, 1 Tbsp jellied cranberry sauce, 1 cup mixed cantaloupe and honeydew melon cubes, 8 oz nonfat milk, 1 cup raw shredded cabbage mixed with 1 Tbsp reduced-fat mayonnaise and 1 Tbsp vinegar, and 4 pecans.

1800 (add 1 1/2 fat exchanges to another meal): 1 serving Broiled Flounder Continental, 1 Tbsp jellied cranberry sauce, 1 cup mixed cantaloupe and honeydew melon cubes, 8 oz nonfat milk, 1 cup raw shredded cabbage mixed with 1 Tbsp reduced-fat mayonnaise and 1 Tbsp vinegar, and 4 pecans.

2000 (add 1 1/2 fat exchanges to another meal): 1 serving Broiled Flounder Continental, 1 Tbsp jellied cranberry sauce, 1 cup mixed cantaloupe and honeydew melon cubes, 8 oz nonfat milk, 1 cup raw shredded cabbage mixed with 1 Tbsp reduced-fat mayonnaise and 1 Tbsp vinegar, and 4 pecans.

This recipe courtesy of the U.S.A. Rice Federation (www.usarice.com).

Broiled Pork Chops with Warm Nectarines

Serving Size: 1/4 recipe, **Total Servings:** 4

1 lb (four 4-oz) loin pork chops,
trimmed of all fat
1/4 tsp coriander seeds
1/4 tsp cumin
1/2 tsp freshly ground black pepper
1/4 cup cider vinegar
1 tsp rum (*optional*)
4 nectarines, pitted, peeled, and
halved

1. Put the pork chops, coriander, cumin, and pepper in a zippered plastic bag and add the vinegar and optional rum. Fasten the bag and place in the refrigerator for 8 hours or overnight to marinate. When ready to cook, preheat a broiler. Place the chops on a broiling pan, along with the nectarines. Place the pan about 6 inches below the heat source. Broil 3–4 minutes per side. Remove and serve hot.

EXCHANGES
1 Fruit	3 Lean Meat

Calories	217
Calories from Fat	69
Total Fat	8 g
Saturated Fat	2.6 g
Polyunsaturated Fat	0.6 g
Monounsaturated Fat	3.4 g
Cholesterol	58 mg
Sodium	47 mg
Total Carbohydrate	15 g
Dietary Fiber	2 g
Sugars	12 g
Protein	23 g

FITTING YOUR PLAN

CALORIE PLAN

1500 (borrow 1 meat exchange from breakfast): 1 serving Broiled Pork Chops with Warm Nectarines, 1 cup mixed raw nonstarchy salad vegetables, 1/2 cup steamed asparagus, 1/2 cup corn, 3/4 oz pretzels, 1 cup nonfat milk, 2 Tbsp reduced-fat salad dressing, and 1 tsp margarine.

1800 1 serving Broiled Pork Chops with Warm Nectarines, 1 cup mixed raw nonstarchy vegetables, 1/2 cup steamed asparagus, 1/2 cup corn, 3/4 oz pretzels, 1 cup nonfat milk, 2 Tbsp reduced-fat salad dressing, and 1 tsp margarine.

2000 1 serving Broiled Pork Chops with Warm Nectarines, 1 cup mixed raw nonstarchy vegetables, 1/2 cup steamed asparagus, 1/2 cup corn, 3/4 oz pretzels, 1 cup nonfat milk, 2 Tbsp reduced-fat salad dressing, and 1 tsp margarine.

This recipe courtesy of the California Tree Fruit Agreement (www.eatcaliforniafruit.com).

Burgundy Beef and Vegetable Stew

Serving Size: 1/6 recipe, **Total Servings:** 6

1 1/2 lb beef eye round
1 Tbsp vegetable oil
1 tsp dried thyme leaves
1/2 tsp salt
1/2 tsp pepper
1 can (13 3/4 oz) ready-to-serve beef broth
1/2 cup Burgundy wine
3 large cloves garlic, crushed
1 1/2 cups baby carrots
1 cup frozen whole pearl onions
2 Tbsp cornstarch, dissolved in 2 Tbsp water
1 pkg (8 oz) frozen sugar snap peas

1. Trim fat from the beef and cut into 1-inch pieces.

2. In a Dutch oven, heat oil over medium-high heat until hot. Add beef (half at a time) and brown evenly, stirring occasionally. Pour off drippings. Season with thyme, salt, and pepper. Stir in broth, wine, and garlic. Bring to a boil; reduce heat to low. Cover tightly and simmer for 1 1/2 hours.

3. Add carrots and onions. Cover and continue cooking for 35–40 minutes or until beef and vegetables are tender.

4. Bring beef stew to a boil over medium-high heat. Add cornstarch mixture; cook and stir 1 minute. Stir in sugar snap peas.

5. Reduce heat to medium and cook for 3–4 minutes or until peas are heated through.

EXCHANGES

2 Vegetable   3 Lean Meat

Calories	220
Calories from Fat	55
Total Fat	6 g
Saturated Fat	1.4 g
Polyunsaturated Fat	0.9 g
Monounsaturated Fat	2.9 g
Cholesterol	50 mg
Sodium	567 mg
Total Carbohydrate	11 g
Dietary Fiber	3 g
Sugars	5 g
Protein	29 g

FITTING YOUR PLAN

CALORIE PLAN	
1500	(borrow 1 meat exchange from breakfast): 1 serving Burgundy Beef and Vegetable Stew, 2/3 cup egg noodles, 2 small tangerines, 8 oz nonfat milk, and 8 pecan halves.
1800	1 serving Burgundy Beef and Vegetable Stew, 2/3 cup egg noodles, 2 small tangerines, 8 oz nonfat milk, and 8 pecan halves.
2000	1 serving Burgundy Beef and Vegetable Stew, 2/3 cup egg noodles, 2 small tangerines, 8 oz nonfat milk, and 8 pecan halves.

This recipe courtesy of the Texas Beef Council (www.txbeef.org).

Calabrian Pork Stovetop Stew

Serving Size: 1/4 recipe, **Total Servings:** 4

1 lb lean pork, cut into 3/4-inch cubes (shoulder, fresh leg, tenderloin)
2 Tbsp flour
1 Tbsp olive oil
3 medium carrots, pared and sliced 1/2 inch thick
2 cloves garlic, crushed
1 can (14 1/2 oz) diced tomatoes
1/2 cup dry red wine
1 tsp Italian seasoning
1/4 tsp salt
1/4 tsp black pepper
1/8 tsp cayenne
1 cup frozen pearl onions
1 pkg (9 oz) Italian green beans

1. Toss pork cubes with flour and brown in hot oil in a large skillet with lid. Remove pork and reserve. Sauté carrots in skillet, adding more olive oil if necessary, until brightly colored; return pork to pan with garlic, tomatoes, wine, Italian seasoning, salt, pepper, and cayenne. Bring to a boil, lower heat, cover, and simmer for 20 minutes, until pork and carrots are tender. Stir in onions and green beans and heat through, about 5–7 minutes.

EXCHANGES

1/2 Starch	3 Lean Meat	3 Vegetable

Calories	264
Calories from Fat	71
Total Fat	8 g
Saturated Fat	1.9 g
Polyunsaturated Fat	0.9 g
Monounsaturated Fat	4.1 g
Cholesterol	66 mg
Sodium	446 mg
Total Carbohydrate	21 g
Dietary Fiber	5 g
Sugars	11 g
Protein	27 g

FITTING YOUR PLAN

CALORIE PLAN

1500 (borrow 1 meat exchange from breakfast and 1 vegetable exchange from a snack. You have an extra 1/2 starch exchange for another meal in the day): 1 serving Calabrian Pork Stovetop Stew, 1 (1 oz) slice rye bread, 8 oz nonfat milk, 1/2 cup mango fruit, and 2 tsp tub margarine.

1800 (borrow 1 vegetable exchange from a snack. You have an extra 1/2 starch exchange for another meal in the day): 1 serving Calabrian Pork Stovetop Stew, 1 (1 oz) slice rye bread, 8 oz nonfat milk, 1/2 cup mango fruit, and 2 tsp tub margarine.

2000 (borrow 1 vegetable exchange from a snack. You have an extra 1/2 starch exchange for another meal in the day): 1 serving Calabrian Pork Stovetop Stew, 1 (1 oz) slice rye bread, 8 oz nonfat milk, 1/2 cup mango fruit, and 2 tsp tub margarine.

This recipe courtesy of the National Pork Board (www.porkandhealth.org).

Caramelized Salmon with Cherry Salsa

Serving Size: 1/6 recipe, **Total Servings:** 6

1 1/2 lb fresh or frozen salmon fillet with skin

3 Tbsp brown sugar

1 Tbsp grated orange peel

1/2 tsp coarsely ground pepper

1 ripe mango or papaya, seeded, peeled, and chopped

1 cup frozen tart cherries, thawed, drained, and halved (or 1/2 cup dried tart cherries)

2 Tbsp chopped fresh mint, basil, or cilantro

2 tsp balsamic vinegar

1/4 tsp crushed red pepper

1. Thaw fish, if frozen. Stir together brown sugar, orange peel, and pepper. Place fish, skin side down, in a shallow pan. Rub sugar mixture over fish. Cover and refrigerate 2–8 hours.

2. Remove fish from pan, draining off any juices. Place salmon, skin side down, on gas grill over medium heat or on charcoal grill 4–6 inches from medium-hot coals. Grill for 20–25 minutes or until fish flakes easily. Do not turn fish.

3. Meanwhile, toss together mango or papaya, cherries, mint, vinegar, and red pepper. Spoon fruit salsa over warm fish. Serve immediately.

Note: To bake salmon instead of grilling, spray a baking dish with nonstick cooking spray. Put salmon, skin side down, in pan. Rub with sugar mixture. Cover with foil and refrigerate 2–8 hours. Bake, covered, in a preheated 350°F oven for 25 minutes. Remove cover and bake 5–10 minutes or until fish flakes easily. Prepare fruit salsa as directed above. Spoon over warm fish. Serve immediately.

EXCHANGES*

1 Fruit	1/2 Fat	3 Lean Meat

Calories	263
Calories from Fat	90
Total Fat	10 g
Saturated Fat	1.7 g
Polyunsaturated Fat	2.2 g
Monounsaturated Fat	4.8 g
Cholesterol	77 mg
Sodium	62 mg
Total Carbohydrate	17 g
Dietary Fiber	1 g
Sugars	15 g
Protein	25 g

*Values are for eating the fish without the skin.

FITTING YOUR PLAN

CALORIE PLAN	
1500	(borrow 1 lean-meat exchange from breakfast): 1 serving Caramelized Salmon with Cherry Salsa, 2/3 cup brown rice, 8 oz nonfat milk, 1 cup steamed broccoli, and 1 1/2 tsp margarine.
1800	1 serving Caramelized Salmon with Cherry Salsa, 2/3 cup brown rice, 8 oz nonfat milk, 1 cup steamed broccoli, and 1 1/2 tsp margarine.
2000	1 serving Caramelized Salmon with Cherry Salsa, 2/3 cup brown rice, 8 oz nonfat milk, 1 cup steamed broccoli, and 1 1/2 tsp margarine.

This recipe courtesy of the Cherry Marketing Institute (www.usacherries.com).

Chicken Waldorf Pitas with Curried Yogurt Sauce

Serving Size: 1/8 recipe, **Total Servings:** 8

Curried Yogurt Sauce
2 whole chicken breasts (1 lb), skinned, boned, cooked, and cubed
1/2 cup fat-free Italian dressing
1 medium green apple, cubed
1/4 cup thinly sliced celery
2 oz sliced almonds, toasted
3 Tbsp raisins
2 California avocados, seeded, peeled, and cubed
4 pita breads, halved (5 1/4-inch breads)
8 pieces curly green leaf lettuce
1 cup cherry tomatoes (*optional*)

Curried Yogurt Sauce

1 cup plain nonfat yogurt
1/2 to 1 tsp curry powder
1/4 tsp mace

Stir ingredients together.

1. Prepare Curried Yogurt Sauce.

2. Marinate chicken in Italian dressing for 4–8 hours. Stir in apple, celery, almonds, and raisins. Add Curried Yogurt Sauce. Gently fold in avocados. Place lettuce in pita halves and fill with chicken mixture. Garnish with tomatoes.

EXCHANGES

1 Starch	2 Very Lean Meat
1 Carbohydrate	2 Fat

Calories	323
Calories from Fat	122
Total Fat	14 g
Saturated Fat	2.0 g
Polyunsaturated Fat	2.4 g
Monounsaturated Fat	7.8 g
Cholesterol	35 mg
Sodium	383 mg
Total Carbohydrate	33 g
Dietary Fiber	5 g
Sugars	9 g
Protein	20 g

FITTING YOUR PLAN

When this recipe is used, you have an extra 4–6 g of fat (approximately 1 fat exchange) because it contains very-lean-meat exchanges instead of lean-meat exchanges. The fruit exchange is used as the carbohydrate exchange.

1500   1 serving Chicken Waldorf Pitas with Curried Yogurt Sauce, 1/2 cup green peas, 1 cup nonfat milk, 2 cups raw nonstarchy vegetables (e.g., lettuce, carrots, cucumbers), and 2 Tbsp reduced-fat salad dressing.

1800   (you have an extra 1 lean-meat exchange for another meal in the day): 1 serving Chicken Waldorf Pitas with Curried Yogurt Sauce, 1/2 cup green peas, 1 cup nonfat milk, 2 cups raw nonstarchy vegetables (e.g., lettuce, carrots, cucumbers), and 2 Tbsp reduced-fat salad dressing.

2000   (you have an extra 1 lean-meat exchange for another meal in the day): 1 serving Chicken Waldorf Pitas with Curried Yogurt Sauce, 1/2 cup green peas, 1 cup nonfat milk, 2 cups raw nonstarchy vegetables (e.g., lettuce, carrots, cucumbers), and 2 Tbsp reduced-fat salad dressing.

This recipe courtesy of the California Avocado Commission (www.avocado.org).

Chicken with Wine-Basted Grapes

Serving Size: 1/2 recipe, **Total Servings:** 2

2 (3 oz each) boneless, skinless
chicken breasts or fish fillets
2 tsp olive oil
1 Tbsp shallots, thinly sliced
1/2 tsp dried thyme leaves, crushed
1 cup California seedless grapes,
halved
1/4 cup dry white wine
Salt and pepper to taste

1. Sprinkle chicken★ or fish with salt
and pepper. Heat oil in a frying pan
and brown on each side. Remove to
baking dish and bake 12 minutes at
375°F. Sauté shallots in pan drippings.
Stir in 1/2 tsp salt (optional), thyme,
dash pepper, and wine. Gently boil
2 minutes or until liquid is reduced
by half. Add grapes and boil 1 minute
longer. Remove from heat and serve
grape sauce over chicken.

★For grilled chicken, prepare sauce by sautéing shallots in olive oil, then completing the sauce as above.

EXCHANGES
1 Fruit   1 Fat   3 Very Lean Meat

Calories	212
Calories from Fat	65
Total Fat	7 g
Saturated Fat	1.4 g
Polyunsaturated Fat	1.0 g
Monounsaturated Fat	4.1 g
Cholesterol	52 mg
Sodium	630 mg
Total Carbohydrate	15 g
Dietary Fiber	1 g
Sugars	12 g
Protein	20 g

FITTING YOUR PLAN

Very lean meat has 0–1 g of fat per ounce, and lean meat has 3 g of fat per ounce. Using this recipe, you have an extra 6–9 g of fat per ounce (or approximately 1 1/2 fat exchanges) for this meal.

CALORIE PLAN

1500 (borrow 1 meat exchange from breakfast): 1 serving Chicken with Wine-Basted Grapes, 2/3 cup cooked couscous or pasta, 8 oz nonfat milk, 1 cup mixed cooked broccoli and cauliflower, 1 tsp tub margarine, and 9 mixed nuts.

1800 1 serving Chicken with Wine-Basted Grapes, 2/3 cup cooked couscous or pasta, 8 oz nonfat milk, 1 cup mixed cooked broccoli and cauliflower, 1 tsp tub margarine, and 9 mixed nuts.

2000 1 serving Chicken with Wine-Basted Grapes, 2/3 cup cooked couscous or pasta, 8 oz nonfat milk, 1 cup mixed cooked broccoli and cauliflower, 1 tsp tub margarine, and 9 mixed nuts.

This recipe courtesy of the California Table Grape Commission (www.freshCaliforniagrapes.com).

Curried Pumpkin Peanut Soup

Serving Size: 3/4 cup, **Total Servings:** 6

1 1/2 cups chopped, peeled apple
    1 cup onion, chopped
  1/4 cup dry sherry, apple juice, or
     water
1 1/2 tsp curry powder
    1 can (15 oz) pure pumpkin
    1 can (14 1/2 oz) reduced-
     sodium chicken broth
  1/4 cup creamy peanut butter
  3/4 cup evaporated nonfat milk
     Garnishes (*optional*): chopped
     peanuts, chopped red-skinned
     apple, fresh cilantro, and/or hot
     pepper seasoning.

1. Combine apple, onion, and sherry in a large saucepan over medium–high heat. Cook, stirring occasionally, until onion is soft and most of sherry evaporates, about 8 minutes. Add curry powder and stir until fragrant, about 30 seconds. Stir in pumpkin, broth, and peanut butter. Cover, bring to a boil, reduce heat, and simmer gently for 10 minutes. Stir in milk. Cool.

2. Whirl in blender or food processor until smooth. (Chill soup if prepared ahead.) Reheat gently to serve. Garnish as desired.

EXCHANGES
1 Carbohydrate   1 Medium-Fat Meat

Calories	154
Calories from Fat	55
Total Fat	6 g
Saturated Fat	1.2 g
Polyunsaturated Fat	1.7 g
Monounsaturated Fat	2.7 g
Cholesterol	0 mg
Sodium	556 mg
Total Carbohydrate	19 g
Dietary Fiber	4 g
Sugars	12 g
Protein	7 g

FITTING YOUR PLAN

Lean meats have 3 g of fat per ounce and medium-fat meats have 5 g of fat per ounce. For one serving of this soup, you need to take away 2 g of fat from the meal (approximately 1/2 fat exchange). The fat-free milk exchange is counted in the meal for the carbohydrate below.

CALORIE PLAN

1500   1 serving Curried Pumpkin Peanut Soup, 1 slice (1 oz) pumpernickel bread, 1/2 cup corn, 17 small grapes, 1 cup cooked broccoli and cauliflower mix, 1 oz lean meat or cheese, lettuce, and 1 1/2 tsp low-fat mayonnaise.

1800   1 serving Curried Pumpkin Peanut Soup, 1 slice (1 oz) pumpernickel bread, 1/2 cup corn, 17 small grapes, 1 cup cooked broccoli and cauliflower mix, 2 oz lean meat or cheese, lettuce, and 1 1/2 tsp low-fat mayonnaise.

2000   1 serving Curried Pumpkin Peanut Soup, 1 slice (1 oz) pumpernickel bread, 1/2 cup corn, 17 small grapes, 1 cup cooked broccoli and cauliflower mix, 2 oz lean meat or cheese, lettuce, and 1 1/2 tsp low-fat mayonnaise.

This recipe courtesy of the National Peanut Board (www.nationalpeanutboard.org).

Curried Rice Egg Salad

Serving Size: 1/6 recipe, **Total Servings:** 6

1 pkg (12 oz) long-grain and wild rice
6 hard cooked eggs
1 cup (8 oz) plain low-fat yogurt
1 1/2 to 2 tsp curry powder
2 cups fresh broccoli (about 8 oz), chopped
6 large tomatoes
Spinach leaves (*optional*)

1. Cook rice according to package directions. Set aside. Slice one egg, reserving two center slices for garnish. Chop remaining eggs.

2. Stir together yogurt and curry powder until well blended. Stir in reserved rice, chopped eggs, and broccoli. Chill to blend flavors. Just before serving, cut each tomato into six sections and place on spinach leaves, if desired. Top each with about 1 1/2 cups egg salad mixture. Garnish with reserved halved egg slices.

EXCHANGES

3 Starch   1 Medium-Fat Meat
2 Vegetable

Calories 343	
Calories from Fat 62	
Total Fat . . . . 7 g	
Saturated Fat . . . . 1.9 g	
Polyunsaturated Fat . . . . 1.1 g	
Monounsaturated Fat . . . . 2.3 g	
Cholesterol . . . . 214 mg	
Sodium . . . . 758 mg	
Total Carbohydrate . . . . 56 g	
Dietary Fiber . . . . 4 g	
Sugars . . . . 9 g	
Protein . . . . 17 g	

FITTING YOUR PLAN

This recipe uses 1 medium-fat-meat exchange. Lean meats have 3 g of fat per ounce, and medium-fat meats have 5 g of fat per ounce. You need to take away 2 g of fat (approximately 1/2 fat exchange from a meal) when using this recipe.

CALORIE PLAN

1500 (borrow 1 starch exchange from another meal or snack in the day, but give 1 oz lean meat to another meal): 1 serving Curried Rice Egg Salad, 12 sweet cherries, 6 oz 100-calorie yogurt, and 6 pecan halves.

1800 (borrow 1 starch exchange from another meal or snack in the day, but give 2 oz lean meat to another meal): 1 serving Curried Rice Egg Salad, 12 sweet cherries, 6 oz 100-calorie yogurt, and 6 pecan halves.

2000 (borrow 1 starch exchange from another meal or snack in the day, but give 2 oz lean meat to another meal): 1 serving Curried Rice Egg Salad, 12 sweet cherries, 6 oz 100-calorie yogurt, and 6 pecan halves.

This recipe courtesy of the American Egg Board (www.aeb.org).

East Indian Chicken Kabobs in an Orange Yogurt Marinade

Serving Size: 1/4 recipe, **Total Servings:** 4

2/3 cup plain nonfat yogurt
　2 seedless oranges, divided
　　Salt and freshly ground pepper
　4 (3 oz each) chicken breasts,
　　skinned and boned
　2 Tbsp freshly grated horseradish
　　Garnish: 1 of the 2 oranges,
　　peeled and divided into
　　sections
　　Boston Bibb lettuce leaves

1. In a small bowl, combine 3 Tbsp of yogurt with the juice and grated zest of 1 orange and season lightly with salt and pepper. Cut the chicken breasts into 1-inch cubes and marinate in the orange-yogurt mixture. Cover and marinate for 1–2 hours, occasionally turning the chicken pieces to coat evenly with the marinade.

2. Meanwhile, combine the remaining yogurt with the freshly grated horseradish and some black pepper to make a basting mixture. Heat the broiler to medium. Remove the chicken pieces from the marinade and thread the pieces onto four small (6-inch) skewers.

3. Grill the kabobs under medium-high heat on one side for 5 minutes. Turn and baste generously with the horseradish mixture and broil for another 5 minutes. Increase the heat to high, turn the kabobs once again, and brush with horseradish mixture. Broil until the chicken is cooked, about 3–4 more minutes. Serve with a selection of salad leaves and garnish with seedless orange sections.

EXCHANGES

1 Fruit	3 Very Lean Meat

Calories 163
    Calories from Fat 22
Total Fat . . . . 2 g
    Saturated Fat . . . . 0.7 g
    Polyunsaturated Fat . . . . 0.5 g
    Monounsaturated Fat . . . . 0.8 g
Cholesterol . . . . 52 mg
Sodium. . . . . 103 mg
Total Carbohydrate . . . . 14 g
    Dietary Fiber. 2 g
    Sugars . . . . 10 g
Protein . . . . 22 g

FITTING YOUR PLAN

Very lean meats have 0–1 g of fat per ounce, and lean meats have 3 g of fat per ounce. Using this recipe, you have an extra 6–9 g of fat (approximately 1 1/2 fat exchanges).

CALORIE PLAN

1500 (borrow 1 meat exchange from breakfast, but you have an extra 1 1/2 fat exchanges to use in another meal or snack): 1 serving East Indian Chicken Kabobs in an Orange Yogurt Marinade, 2/3 cup cooked rice, 8 oz nonfat milk, 1 cup cooked broccoli, and 2 tsp margarine.

1800 (you have an extra 1 1/2 fat exchanges to use in another meal or snack): 1 serving East Indian Chicken Kabobs in an Orange Yogurt Marinade, 2/3 cup cooked rice, 8 oz nonfat milk, 1 cup cooked broccoli, and 2 tsp margarine.

2000 (you have an extra 1 1/2 fat exchanges to use in another meal or snack): 1 serving East Indian Chicken Kabobs in an Orange Yogurt Marinade, 2/3 cup cooked rice, 8 oz nonfat milk, 1 cup cooked broccoli, and 2 tsp margarine.

This recipe courtesy of the Horseradish Information Council (www.horseradish.org).

Fourth of July Turkey Potato Salad

Serving Size: 1/8 recipe, **Total Servings:** 8

3/4 lb smoked turkey breast, cut into 1/2-inch cubes
1 lb red potatoes, cooked, cut into 1/2-inch cubes
1 cup chopped mild onion
1 cup chopped celery
1 cup chopped red bell pepper
1/2 cup plain nonfat yogurt
1/4 cup light mayonnaise
1/4 cup chopped cilantro
1 Tbsp grainy Dijon-style mustard
1/2 tsp salt (*optional*)
1/2 tsp pepper
Garnish: Fresh cilantro

1. In a medium bowl, combine the turkey, potatoes, onion, celery, and bell pepper.

2. In a small bowl, combine the yogurt, mayonnaise, cilantro, mustard, salt, and pepper. Gently fold into turkey and vegetable mixture. Serve immediately or cover and chill for 1–2 hours. To serve, garnish with fresh cilantro sprigs.

EXCHANGES

1 Starch	1/2 Fat	1 Very Lean Meat

Calories	142
Calories from Fat	29
Total Fat	3 g
Saturated Fat	0.6 g
Polyunsaturated Fat	1.2 g
Monounsaturated Fat	0.9 g
Cholesterol	18 mg
Sodium	692 mg
w/o added salt	547 mg
Total Carbohydrate	17 g
Dietary Fiber	2 g
Sugars	5 g
Protein	12 g

FITTING YOUR PLAN

Because this recipe has a very-lean-meat exchange, an extra 1/2 fat exchange may be added to the meal.

1500   1 serving Fourth of July Turkey Potato Salad, 1 small roll (1 oz), 1 cup mixed blueberries and watermelon, 8 oz nonfat milk, 2 cups raw nonstarchy vegetables, 1 oz low-fat turkey hot dog with less than 3 g of fat per ounce, 2 Tbsp reduced-fat salad dressing, and 6 mixed nuts.

1800   1 serving Fourth of July Turkey Potato Salad, 1 small roll (1 oz), 1 cup mixed blueberries and watermelon, 8 oz nonfat milk, 2 cups raw nonstarchy vegetables, 2 oz low-fat turkey hot dog with less than 3 g of fat per ounce, 2 Tbsp reduced-fat salad dressing, and 6 mixed nuts.

2000   1 serving Fourth of July Turkey Potato Salad, 1 small roll (1 oz), 1 cup mixed blueberries and watermelon, 8 oz nonfat milk, 2 cups raw nonstarchy vegetables, 2 oz low-fat turkey hot dog with less than 3 g of fat per ounce, 2 Tbsp reduced-fat salad dressing, and 6 mixed nuts.

This recipe courtesy of the National Turkey Federation (www.eatturkey.com).

Greek-Style Pocket Sandwiches

Serving Size: 1 sandwich, **Total Servings:** 4

1/4 cup canola oil
  1 Tbsp prepared mustard
1/2 cup lemon juice
  2 cloves garlic, minced
  1 tsp oregano
  1 lb boneless pork loin, well
    trimmed and cut into strips
  1 cup fat-free plain yogurt
  1 cup peeled, chopped cucumber
1/2 clove garlic, crushed
1/2 tsp dill
  2 pita breads, halved
  1 small red onion, thinly sliced

1. Combine canola oil, mustard, lemon juice, garlic, and oregano. Pour over pork strips. Cover and refrigerate for 1–8 hours.

2. Combine yogurt, cucumber, garlic, and dill; cover and refrigerate.

3. Drain marinade from pork strips, removing as much marinade from the meat as possible (use a strainer or colander). Heat oven to 450°F. Place strips in a shallow pan in the oven for 10–12 minutes or until lightly browned. Remove meat from pan with slotted spoon and distribute pork among pita halves. Top each with a generous spoonful of yogurt mixture and some sliced red onion.

EXCHANGES

1 Starch	3 Lean Meat
1/2 Fat	1/2 Fat-Free Milk
1 Vegetable	

Calories	330
Calories from Fat	110
Total Fat	12 g
Saturated Fat	3.0 g
Polyunsaturated Fat	2.0 g
Monounsaturated Fat	6.1 g
Cholesterol	59 mg
Sodium	279 mg
Total Carbohydrate	27 g
Dietary Fiber	2 g
Sugars	6 g
Protein	28 g

FITTING YOUR PLAN

CALORIE PLAN	
1500	(borrow 1 meat exchange from breakfast and give 1/2 milk exchange to another meal): 1 Greek-Style Pocket Sandwich, 1/2 cup green peas, 1/2 cup beets, 1 1/2 tsp tub margarine, and 2 medium fresh figs.
1800	(give 1/2 milk exchange to another meal): 1 Greek-Style Pocket Sandwich, 1/2 cup green peas, 1/2 cup beets, 1 1/2 tsp tub margarine, and 2 medium fresh figs.
2000	(give 1/2 milk exchange to another meal): 1 Greek-Style Pocket Sandwich, 1/2 cup green peas, 1/2 cup beets, 1 1/2 tsp tub margarine, and 2 medium fresh figs.

This recipe courtesy of the Canola Council of Canada (www.canola-council.org).

Grilled Eggplant with Pomegranate Sauce

Serving Size: 1/6 recipe, **Total Servings:** 6

1 large eggplant
2 Tbsp olive oil
3 cloves garlic
1/2 pomegranate syrup★
1/2 tsp salt
Garnish: minced parsley, 1/2 cup pomegranate seeds

★To make pomegranate syrup, in a blender, combine 1/2 cup pomegranate seeds and 1/3 cup sugar.

1. Cut eggplant into 1/4-inch slices and place on paper towels. Sprinkle slices with salt, weigh them down with heavy plates or a board for 30 minutes, then pat them dry with paper towels.

2. Lightly brush with olive oil and place eggplant slices on grill. Grill them for 3 minutes on each side or until they are lightly browned on both sides. Remove from grill and arrange the eggplant overlapping on a serving dish.

3. In a mortar, crush garlic cloves with the salt to a paste. In a non-metallic bowl, combine the garlic paste and pomegranate syrup. Spread a little of the mixture on each eggplant slice. Sprinkle the slices with minced parsley and pomegranate seeds for garnish and chill covered.

EXCHANGES

1 Carbohydrate	1/2 Fat	1 Vegetable

Calories	119
Calories from Fat	42
Total Fat	5 g
Saturated Fat	0.6 g
Polyunsaturated Fat	0.4 g
Monounsaturated Fat	3.3 g
Cholesterol	0 mg
Sodium	396 mg
Total Carbohydrate	20 g
Dietary Fiber	2 g
Sugars	16 g
Protein	1 g

FITTING YOUR PLAN

For the meal patterns below, 1 fruit exchange is counted as the 1 carbohydrate exchange.

CALORIE PLAN

1500 1 serving Grilled Eggplant with Pomegranate Sauce, 2/3 cup brown rice, 8 oz nonfat milk, 1 cup raw mixed nonstarchy vegetables in a salad, 3 Tbsp reduced-fat salad dressing, and 2 oz lean chicken, fish, pork, or beef.

1800 1 serving Grilled Eggplant with Pomegranate Sauce, 2/3 cup brown rice, 8 oz nonfat milk, 1 cup raw mixed nonstarchy vegetables in a salad, 3 Tbsp reduced-fat salad dressing, and 3 oz lean chicken, fish, pork, or beef.

2000 1 serving Grilled Eggplant with Pomegranate Sauce, 2/3 cup brown rice, 8 oz nonfat milk, 1 cup raw mixed nonstarchy vegetables in a salad, 3 Tbsp reduced-fat salad dressing, and 3 oz lean chicken, fish, pork, or beef.

This recipe courtesy of the Pomegranate Council (www.pomegranates.org).

Grilled Georgia Pecan and Cornbread Turkey Burgers

Serving Size: 1/6 recipe, **Total Servings:** 6

1 cup dry cornbread stuffing
1/4 cup water
1 1/4 lb ground turkey
3/4 cup pecans, chopped
3 Tbsp onion, minced
1/2 cup low-fat prepared barbecue sauce
1/4 tsp salt
1 large red onion, thickly sliced
Nonstick cooking spray
5 large leaves green leaf lettuce
5 slices tomato

1. Prepare a hot charcoal fire or preheat a gas grill. In a food processor or blender, combine stuffing and water; process until stuffing becomes coarse crumbs. Transfer to large bowl.

2. Add turkey, pecans, minced onion,  barbecue sauce, and salt to stuffing and mix until well combined. Shape turkey mixture into six patties about 3/4 inch thick. Brush red onion slices and both sides of burgers lightly with nonstick spray. Grill burgers 6–7 minutes on each side or until cooked through. Grill onion slices about 4 minutes on each side.

3. To serve, place one lettuce leaf on each serving plate; top with a burger and a slice of tomato and grilled onion.

EXCHANGES

1/2 Starch	2 Very Lean Meat
1 Vegetable	2 1/2 Fat

Calories 249
    Calories from Fat 111
Total Fat . . . . 12 g
    Saturated Fat . . . . 1.2 g
    Polyunsaturated Fat . . . . 3.5 g
    Monounsaturated Fat . . . . 6.9 g
Cholesterol . . . . 45 mg
Sodium . . . . 405 mg
Total Carbohydrate . . . . 16 g
    Dietary Fiber . . . . 3 g
    Sugars . . . . 5 g
Protein . . . . 19 g

FITTING YOUR PLAN

Very lean meats have 0–1 g of fat per ounce, and lean meats have 3 g of fat per ounce. Therefore, an extra 4–6 g of fat (approximately 1 fat exchange) can be added to this meal.

CALORIE PLAN

1500   1 Grilled Georgia Pecan and Cornbread Turkey Burger, 3/4 cup corn, 1 1/4 cups watermelon, 8 oz nonfat milk, 1 cup raw nonstarchy vegetable salad, 2 Tbsp fat-free Italian salad dressing, and 2 pecan halves on salad.

1800   1 Grilled Georgia Pecan and Cornbread Turkey Burger, 3/4 cup corn, 1 1/4 cups watermelon, 8 oz nonfat milk, 1 cup raw nonstarchy vegetable salad, 2 Tbsp fat-free Italian salad dressing, 2 pecan halves on salad, and 1 oz low-fat cheese.

2000   (borrow 1 fat exchange from midafternoon snack): 1 Grilled Georgia Pecan and Cornbread Turkey Burger, 3/4 cup corn, 1 1/4 cups watermelon, 8 oz nonfat milk, 1 1/2 cups raw nonstarchy vegetable salad, 2 Tbsp fat-free Italian salad dressing, and 1 oz low-fat cheese.

This recipe courtesy of the Georgia Pecan Commission (www.georgiapecans.org).

Honey-Baked Leg of Lamb

Serving Size: 2 oz lamb, **Total Servings:** 20

4 lb American lamb leg, boneless
(or very small American lamb leg)
1/2 cup dry white wine
1/3 cup honey
1/2 cup finely chopped onion
1/2 cup finely chopped fresh mint or
3 Tbsp dried mint
2 Tbsp grated lemon peel
2 Tbsp lemon juice
1 tsp salt
1/2 tsp pepper

1. Combine marinade ingredients. Reserve 1/4 cup for basting.

2. Place lamb in large sealable plastic bag and pour marinade over lamb. Seal tightly and refrigerate 4 hours or overnight. Remove lamb from marinade and discard marinade.

3. Place lamb on rack in baking pan. Bake in 325°F oven for 20–25 minutes per pound or until desired degree of doneness: 160°F for medium or 170°F for well done. Baste.

4. Remove lamb from oven, cover lightly, and let sit for 10 minutes. Internal temperature will rise approximately 10°F.

EXCHANGES
2 Lean Meat

Calories 127
   Calories from Fat 43
Total Fat . . . . 5 g
   Saturated Fat . . . . 1.7 g
   Polyunsaturated Fat . . . . 0.4 g
   Monounsaturated Fat . . . . 1.9 g
Cholesterol . . . . 59 mg
Sodium . . . . 79 mg
Total Carbohydrate . . . . 1 g
   Dietary Fiber . . . . 0 g
   Sugars . . . . 1 g
Protein . . . . 18 g

FITTING YOUR PLAN

CALORIE PLAN	
1500	1 serving Honey-Baked Leg of Lamb, 2/3 cup rice, 3/4 cup mixed blueberries and blackberries, 8 oz nonfat milk, 1 cup cooked greens, 8 black olives, and 1 tsp tub margarine.
1800	3 oz Honey-Baked Leg of Lamb, 2/3 cup rice, 3/4 cup mixed blueberries and blackberries, 8 oz nonfat milk, 1 cup cooked greens, 8 black olives, and 1 tsp tub margarine.
2000	3 oz Honey-Baked Leg of Lamb, 2/3 cup rice, 3/4 cup mixed blueberries and blackberries, 8 oz nonfat milk, 1 cup cooked greens, 8 black olives, and 1 tsp tub margarine.

This recipe courtesy of the American Lamb Board (www.americanlambboard.com).

Japanese Pear Salad

Serving Size: 1/4 recipe, **Total Servings:** 4

2 Tbsp rice vinegar, red wine vinegar, or balsamic vinegar
1 Tbsp packed brown sugar
2 medium fresh USA Anjou or Bosc pears, cored and sliced
1/3 cup thinly sliced mushrooms
1/4 cup each thinly sliced green pepper and radishes
4 Green Onion Brushes

1. Combine vinegar and sugar; gently toss pears in mixture. Allow to stand for 30 minutes to 1 hour to blend flavors; stir occasionally. Drain pears and arrange with vegetables on individual trays or plates.

Green Onion Brushes

Cut a 3-inch piece off the root ends of four medium green onions. Cut three 1-inch lengthwise slashes through the root end; rotate onion a half turn, and make three more 1-inch lengthwise slashes. Place in ice water. Drain before using. Makes 4 brushes.

EXCHANGES
1 Fruit

Calories	64
Calories from Fat	2
Total Fat	0 g
Saturated Fat	0.0 g
Polyunsaturated Fat	0.1 g
Monounsaturated Fat	0.0 g
Cholesterol	0 mg
Sodium	6 mg
Total Carbohydrate	17 g
Dietary Fiber	3 g
Sugars	11 g
Protein	1 g

FITTING YOUR PLAN

CALORIE PLAN	
1500	1 serving Japanese Pear Salad, 2/3 cup rice, 8 oz nonfat milk, 1 cup cooked pea pods, 2 oz lean fish, 1 Tbsp sesame seeds to garnish the pea pods, and 1 tsp margarine.
1800	1 serving Japanese Pear Salad, 2/3 cup rice, 8 oz nonfat milk, 1 cup cooked pea pods, 3 oz lean fish, 1 Tbsp sesame seeds to garnish the pea pods, and 1 tsp margarine.
2000	1 serving Japanese Pear Salad, 2/3 cup rice, 8 oz nonfat milk, 1 cup cooked pea pods, 3 oz lean fish, 1 Tbsp sesame seeds to garnish the pea pods, and 1 tsp margarine.

This recipe courtesy of the Pear Bureau Northwest (www.usapears.com).

Hoppin' John Salad with Toasted Georgia Pecans

Serving Size: 1/6 recipe, **Total Servings:** 6

4 cups thawed frozen black-eyed peas or drained canned black-eyed peas

2 tsp olive oil or pecan oil

1 sweet yellow or red onion, finely chopped

1 red bell pepper, seeded and chopped

1 green bell pepper, seeded and chopped

1 can (14 oz) tomatoes, drained and chopped

3 cloves garlic, minced

1 cup long-grain white rice

2 cups defatted reduced-sodium chicken stock

1 tsp salt or to taste

1/4 tsp cayenne pepper

3/4 cup chopped green onions

1/2 cup chopped toasted pecans
Freshly ground black pepper to taste

1. Drain peas well and set aside.

2. In a large wide saucepan, heat oil over medium heat. Add onions and peppers; stir and cook until softened, about 5 minutes. Add tomatoes and garlic and cook, stirring, for 5 minutes. Add rice and stir for 1 minute to coat the grains. Pour in chicken stock and bring to a simmer. Add salt, cayenne pepper, and reserved black-eyed peas. Cover and simmer on low heat for about 20 minutes or until liquid has been absorbed.

3. To serve, mound on serving plates and shower with green onions, toasted pecans, and black pepper. Serve hot, warm, or cold.

EXCHANGES

| 3 Starch | 1 1/2 Fat | 2 Vegetable |

Calories	363
Calories from Fat	89
Total Fat	10 g
Saturated Fat	0.9 g
Polyunsaturated Fat	2.6 g
Monounsaturated Fat	5.6 g
Cholesterol	0 mg
Sodium.	777 mg
Total Carbohydrate	57 g
Dietary Fiber	11 g
Sugars	8 g
Protein	14 g

FITTING YOUR PLAN

CALORIE PLAN

1500 (borrow 1 starch exchange from midafternoon snack): 1 serving Hoppin' John Salad with Toasted Georgia Pecans, 8 oz nonfat milk, 2 oz lean meat of choice (chicken, beef, or pork), and 1 1/4 cups watermelon cubes.

1800 (borrow 1 starch exchange from midafternoon snack): 1 serving Hoppin' John Salad with Toasted Georgia Pecans, 8 oz nonfat milk, 3 oz lean meat of choice (chicken, beef, or pork), and 1 1/4 cups watermelon cubes.

2000 (borrow 1 starch exchange from midafternoon snack): 1 serving Hoppin' John Salad with Toasted Georgia Pecans, 8 oz nonfat milk, 3 oz lean meat of choice (chicken, beef, or pork), and 1 1/4 cups watermelon cubes.

This recipe courtesy of the Georgia Pecan Commission (www.georgiapecans.org).

Margarita Fruit Salad

Serving Size: 1/8 recipe, **Total Servings:** 8

DRESSING

1/3 cup freshly squeezed lime juice
  2 Tbsp honey
  1 oz tequila (*optional*)
    Pinch of kosher salt
1/4 cup fresh mint, chopped

SALAD

  1 medium fresh California
    Summerwhite peach
  2 medium fresh California peaches
  2 medium fresh California nectarines
  2 medium fresh California plums
  6 California Sugarplums (fresh
    prunes) (*optional*)
  1 cup watermelon, balled or cubed
    Pinch of cayenne pepper
    Lime wedges
    Mint sprigs

1. For the dressing, combine the lime juice, tequila (if desired), and honey in a small bowl and whisk until the honey dissolves. Add a pinch of kosher salt, to taste. Add chopped mint; set aside while cutting the fruit.

2. For the salad, rinse fruit and remove the pits; cut into thin wedges or 1-inch chunks. Combine all fruit in a large bowl; pour dressing over the fruit, stirring gently to distribute. Sprinkle on cayenne pepper and adjust to taste. Serve with a lime wedge and a mint sprig.

EXCHANGES
1 1/2 Fruit

Calories	84
Calories from Fat	4
Total Fat	0 g
Saturated Fat	0.0 g
Polyunsaturated Fat	0.1 g
Monounsaturated Fat	0.1 g
Cholesterol	0 mg
Sodium	2 mg
Total Carbohydrate	21 g
Dietary Fiber	2 g
Sugars	18 g
Protein	1 g

FITTING YOUR PLAN

CALORIE PLAN

1500 (borrow 1/2 fruit exchange from another meal in the day): 1 serving Margarita Fruit Salad, 2/3 cup pasta, 8 oz nonfat milk, 1 cup tomato sauce with 2 oz lean ground chuck or lean ground turkey, and 12 cashews.

1800 (borrow 1/2 fruit exchange from another meal in the day): 1 serving Margarita Fruit Salad, 2/3 cup pasta, 8 oz nonfat milk, 1 cup tomato sauce with 3 oz lean ground chuck or lean ground turkey, and 12 cashews.

2000 (borrow 1/2 fruit exchange from another meal in the day): 1 serving Margarita Fruit Salad, 2/3 cup pasta, 8 oz nonfat milk, 1 cup tomato sauce with 3 oz lean ground chuck or lean ground turkey, and 12 cashews.

This recipe courtesy of the California Tree Fruit Agreement (www.eatcaliforniafruit.com).

Mediterranean Burger

Serving Size: 1 sandwich, **Total Servings:** 4

1/2 tsp oregano, ground
1/2 tsp garlic powder
1/2 tsp ground black pepper
1/2 tsp salt
1/4 tsp onion powder
1/4 tsp ground cumin
  1 lb fresh ground lean American lamb
2/3 cup plain low-fat yogurt
1/2 medium cucumber, peeled, seeded, and chopped
  2 green onions, thinly sliced
  2 tsp dried mint
1/2 tsp sugar
  2 whole-wheat pita bread rounds (6 1/2 inches each), halved crosswise and split
  1 cup fresh spinach or lettuce, chopped

1. Combine seasonings; stir in lamb; mix well. Divide into six 4-oz portions. Shape into patties. Broil or grill to desired doneness.

2. For sauce, combine yogurt, cucumber, onion, mint, and sugar. To serve, fill pita halves with meat, sauce, and spinach.

Note: Ground meat should be cooked to at least 160°F.

EXCHANGES
1 Starch   3 Lean Meat   1 Vegetable

Calories	265
Calories from Fat	78
Total Fat	9 g
Saturated Fat	3.0 g
Polyunsaturated Fat	0.8 g
Monounsaturated Fat	3.5 g
Cholesterol	72 mg
Sodium	455 mg
Total Carbohydrate	21 g
Dietary Fiber	2 g
Sugars	4 g
Protein	27 g

FITTING YOUR PLAN

CALORIE PLAN

1500 (borrow 1 lean-meat exchange from breakfast): 1 serving Mediterranean Burger, 1/2 cup cooked peas, 3/4 cup mixed blackberries and melon, 8 oz nonfat milk, 1 cup mixed salad vegetables, 2 Tbsp reduced-fat salad dressing, and 6 mixed nuts.

1800 1 serving Mediterranean Burger, 1/2 cup cooked peas, 3/4 cup mixed blackberries and melon, 8 oz nonfat milk, 1 cup mixed salad vegetables, 2 Tbsp reduced-fat salad dressing, and 6 mixed nuts.

2000 1 serving Mediterranean Burger, 1/2 cup cooked peas, 3/4 cup mixed blackberries and melon, 8 oz nonfat milk, 1 cup mixed salad vegetables, 2 Tbsp reduced-fat salad dressing, and 6 mixed nuts.

This recipe courtesy of the American Lamb Board (www.americanlambboard.com).

Mediterranean Stuffed Tomatoes

Serving Size: 1/6 recipe, **Total Servings:** 6

12 large tomatoes
1 tsp salt

FILLING

1 Tbsp canola oil
3/4 lb 95% lean ground beef
1 cup (1 medium) yellow onion, diced to 1/4-inch pieces
1/2 cup red bell pepper, diced to 1/4-inch pieces
2 tsp garlic, freshly minced
1 cup basmati rice or long-grain rice
1 tsp salt
1/8 tsp cayenne pepper, ground
1 cup tomatoes, chopped
1 oz pine nuts, toasted
3 Tbsp dill, freshly minced
2 Tbsp mint, freshly minced
2 Tbsp oregano, freshly minced
1/4 cup dried cranberries, chopped
3 Tbsp lemon juice, fresh
2 3/4 cups low-sodium beef or chicken broth

1. Preheat oven to 350°F.

2. Cut tops off of tomatoes about 3/4 inch down from top. Save for "lids." Using a spoon or melon baller, scoop out insides of tomatoes, leaving outer layer intact. Discard insides, or you can discard seeds, and save pulp for use in filling, if desired. Sprinkle inside of tomatoes with salt and invert onto rack to drain. This will make the tomatoes firmer for baking. Let sit inverted while you prepare the filling, at least 20 minutes.

TO PREPARE FILLING

3. Over high heat, brown the beef and onions in oil and cook until golden brown, 8–10 minutes.

4. Add red bell pepper, garlic, rice, salt, and cayenne pepper and stir in. Let cook 2 minutes.

5. Add remaining ingredients and bring to a boil. Stir; then reduce heat to simmer and cover.

6. Let cook for 10–15 minutes, until liquid is just absorbed. Rice will still be a little chewy.

7. Stuff hollowed out tomatoes with about 1/2 cup of filling each, mounding slightly on top. Place in a large baking dish; the tomatoes should just touch each other in the pan. Place tomato top "lids" back on tomatoes. Cover with foil and place in preheated oven. Bake for 30–40 minutes until hot throughout, but tomatoes should still hold their shape.

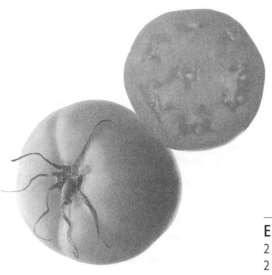

EXCHANGES

2 Starch	2 Lean Meat
2 Vegetable	1/2 Fat

Calories 347
    Calories from Fat 90
Total Fat . . . . 10 g
    Saturated Fat . . . . 2.5 g
    Polyunsaturated Fat . . . . 2.3 g
    Monounsaturated Fat . . . . 4.2 g
Cholesterol . . . . 49 mg
Sodium. . . . . 901 mg
Total Carbohydrate . . . . 43 g
    Dietary Fiber. 4 g
    Sugars . . . . 12 g
Protein . . . . 23 g

FITTING YOUR PLAN

CALORIE PLAN

1500   1 serving Mediterranean Stuffed Tomatoes, 8 dried apricot halves, 8 oz nonfat milk, and 12 black olives.

1800   (give 1 lean-meat exchange to another meal): 1 serving Mediterranean Stuffed Tomatoes, 8 dried apricot halves, 8 oz nonfat milk, and 12 black olives.

2000   (give 1 lean-meat exchange to another meal): 1 serving Mediterranean Stuffed Tomatoes, 8 dried apricot halves, 8 oz nonfat milk, and 12 black olives.

This recipe courtesy of the California Tomato Commission (www.tomato.org).

Orange-Sauced Beef

Serving Size: 1/4 recipe, **Total Servings:** 4

12 oz boneless beef top round steak
 1 Tbsp all-purpose flour
1/2 tsp dry mustard
1/4 tsp salt
1/4 tsp pepper
       Nonstick cooking spray
 1 medium onion, sliced
3/4 cup frozen Florida orange juice
       concentrate, thawed
1/2 cup water
 2 Tbsp vinegar
 4 gingersnaps, crushed
       Hot cooked noodles (*optional*)
       Florida orange slice twists
          (*optional*)
       Sprigs of fresh sage (*optional*)

1. Trim fat from beef. Partially freeze beef. Thinly slice beef across the grain into bite-size strips. In a bowl or plastic bag, combine flour, mustard, salt, and pepper. Add meat; toss to coat well.

2. Spray an unheated large skillet with nonstick cooking spray. Preheat over medium heat. Brown beef in skillet over medium heat. Remove skillet from heat.

3. Carefully add onion, thawed concentrate, water, and vinegar to skillet. Bring to boiling; reduce heat. Cover and simmer about 15 minutes or until beef is tender. Add gingersnaps. Cook and stir for 4–5 minutes or until slightly thickened. If desired, serve over noodles and garnish with orange slices and sage.

Give It a Twist

Garnishes of Florida orange slice twists are as easy to make as they are attractive. To make twists, thinly slice an unpeeled Florida orange. Make one cut from the edge to the center of the slice. Twist the ends in opposite directions. If desired, twist two thin slices together.

EXCHANGES

1 Starch	2 Lean Meat	1 Fruit

Calories 233
    Calories from Fat 42
Total Fat . . . . 5 g
    Saturated Fat . . . . 1.3 g
    Polyunsaturated Fat . . . . 0.3 g
    Monounsaturated Fat . . . . 2.1 g
Cholesterol . . . . 44 mg
Sodium . . . . 216 mg
Total Carbohydrate . . . . 31 g
    Dietary Fiber . . . . 1 g
    Sugars . . . . 24 g
Protein . . . . 17 g

FITTING YOUR PLAN

CALORIE PLAN	
1500	1 serving Orange-Sauced Beef, 1/3 cup cooked noodles, 8 oz nonfat milk, 1/2 cup cooked broccoli, 1/2 cup cooked red cabbage, 1 tsp olive oil on cabbage, and 6 mixed nuts.
1800	(save 1 lean-meat exchange for another meal or snack): 1 serving Orange-Sauced Beef, 1/3 cup cooked noodles, 8 oz nonfat milk, 1/2 cup cooked broccoli, 1/2 cup cooked red cabbage, 1 tsp olive oil on cabbage, and 6 mixed nuts.
2000	(save 1 lean-meat exchange for another meal or snack): 1 serving Orange-Sauced Beef, 1/3 cup cooked noodles, 8 oz nonfat milk, 1/2 cup cooked broccoli, 1/2 cup cooked red cabbage, 1 tsp olive oil on cabbage, and 6 mixed nuts.

This recipe courtesy of the Florida Department of Citrus (www.floridajuice.com).

Oven-Roasted Fish Fillets in White Wine with Hazelnuts

Serving Size: 1/8 recipe, **Total Servings:** 8

2 large garlic cloves, coarsely chopped (1 Tbsp)

3/4 lb yellow onions, coarsely chopped (2 cups)

1/2 cup extra-virgin olive oil
Sea salt

1/4 tsp ground red chili pepper

1 tsp fennel seeds

2 bay leaves

2 cups dry white wine

1 Tbsp finely grated orange zest

1/3 cup salted capers, carefully rinsed and drained (*optional*)

1 lb potatoes, peeled and cut into small cubes

1 cup chopped, drained canned tomatoes

1 tsp dried thyme or dried Sicilian or Greek oregano (rigani)

2 lb thick fish fillets

1/3 cup dried unseasoned bread crumbs

1/3 cup finely chopped blanched hazelnuts

1. Combine the garlic and onions in a large, heavy sauté pan with 1/4 cup of the oil and 1 tsp salt. Set over medium-low heat and cook gently, stirring often, until the onions are very soft and almost melting in the oil. Add the chili pepper, fennel seeds, and bay leaves and mix well. Pour in the wine and continue cooking at a low simmer for 15–20 minutes, until the wine has reduced by almost half. Remove the pan from the heat and stir in the grated orange zest and, if you wish, the capers. Set aside.

2. Bring a small pot of lightly salted water to a rolling bowl and drop in the potatoes. Boil vigorously for 5 minutes; then drain immediately and transfer to a small bowl. Stir in 2 Tbsp of the remaining olive oil and the tomatoes and stir to mix well.

3. Preheat the oven to 350°F.

4. Distribute the potatoes and tomatoes over the bottom of a rectangular or oval oven dish large enough to hold all of the ingredients. Sprinkle with the dried thyme, crumbling the herb between your fingers. Lay the fish fillets on top of the potatoes, and then spoon the wine sauce over the fish, covering it with the sauce. Sprinkle liberally with the breadcrumbs and chopped hazelnuts and dribble the remaining 2 Tbsp of olive oil over the top.

5. Cover the dish with aluminum foil. Bake for 20 minutes; then raise the heat to 450°F, remove the foil, and bake an additional 10 minutes or until the surface is crisp and brown. Serve immediately.

EXCHANGES

1 Starch	3 Very Lean Meat
1 Vegetable	3 Fat

Calories 338
    Calories from Fat 159
Total Fat . . . . 18 g
    Saturated Fat . . . . 2.2 g
    Polyunsaturated Fat. . . . . 1.9 g
    Monounsaturated Fat . . . . 12.3 g
Cholesterol . . . . 65 mg
Sodium. . . . . 182 mg
Total Carbohydrate . . . . 18 g
    Dietary Fiber. 3 g
    Sugars . . . . 5 g
Protein . . . . 24 g

Perfect this Meal

Choose thick, meaty fillets from a fish such as haddock or red snapper, and use a dry but flowery wine, such as sauvignon blanc, a vermentino from Sardinia, or a white from the Languedoc region of southern France.

FITTING YOUR PLAN

Because this recipe has 3 very-lean-meat exchanges and the meal pattern is based on lean-meat exchanges, an extra 6–9 g of fat (about 1 1/2 fat exchanges) may be added.

CALORIE PLAN

1500   (borrow 1 lean-meat exchange from breakfast): 1 serving Oven-Roasted Fish Fillets in White Wine with Hazelnuts, 1 slice (1 oz) rye bread, 1/2 cup fresh fruit salad, 8 oz nonfat milk, 1 cup mixed vegetable raw salad, 1 tsp low-fat margarine, and 2 Tbsp fat-free Italian salad dressing.

1800   1 serving Oven-Roasted Fish Fillets in White Wine with Hazelnuts, 1 slice (1 oz) rye bread, 1/2 cup fresh fruit salad, 8 oz nonfat milk, 1 cup mixed vegetable raw salad, 1 tsp low-fat margarine, and 2 Tbsp fat-free Italian salad dressing.

2000   1 serving Oven-Roasted Fish Fillets in White Wine with Hazelnuts, 1 slice (1 oz) rye bread, 1/2 cup fresh fruit salad, 8 oz nonfat milk, 1 cup mixed vegetable raw salad, 1 tsp low-fat margarine, and 2 Tbsp fat-free Italian salad dressing.

This recipe courtesy of the Hazelnut Council (www.hazelnutcouncil.org).

Pecos Pitas with Pistachios

Serving Size: 1/8 recipe, **Total Servings:** 8

1 can (11 oz) Mexicorn, drained
2 medium zucchini, diced (1/2 lb)
1–2 Tbsp canned diced green chilies
  (or jalapenos, if preferred)
1 cup coarsely chopped California
  pistachios
  Cumin Vinaigrette
4 pita pocket breads
  Iceberg lettuce leaves
1 large tomato, thinly sliced
1 cup canned black beans or red
  kidney beans

1. Toss corn, zucchini, chilies, and 3/4 cup pistachios together with half the Cumin Vinaigrette. Warm pita pockets in 350°F oven for about 3 minutes, then halve and fill each half with lettuce, tomato slices, and 1/3 cup corn mixture. Add a spoonful of beans to each. Place on plates; drizzle remaining dressing over filling and sprinkle with remaining pistachios.

Cumin Vinaigrette

1/4 cup vegetable oil
1/4 cup cider vinegar
  1 Tbsp sugar
  1 tsp cumin seed

Combine all ingredients in a measuring cup. Stir vigorously to blend.

EXCHANGES

2 Starch	3 Fat	1 Vegetable

Calories	320
Calories from Fat	147
Total Fat	16 g
Saturated Fat	1.8 g
Polyunsaturated Fat	3.7 g
Monounsaturated Fat	9.9 g
Cholesterol	0 mg
Sodium	365 mg
Total Carbohydrate	37 g
Dietary Fiber	5 g
Sugars	7 g
Protein	8 g

FITTING YOUR PLAN

CALORIE PLAN

1500   (borrow 1 fat exchange from another meal): 1 serving Pecos Pitas with Pistachios, 1/3 of a small cantaloupe, 8 oz nonfat milk, 1/2 cup cooked green beans, and 1/2 cup 4.5% fat cottage cheese.

1800   (borrow 1 fat exchange from another meal): 1 serving Pecos Pitas with Pistachios, 1/3 of a small cantaloupe, 8 oz nonfat milk, 1/2 cup cooked green beans, and 3/4 cup 4.5% fat cottage cheese.

2000   (borrow 1 fat exchange from another meal): 1 serving Pecos Pitas with Pistachios, 1/3 of a small cantaloupe, 8 oz nonfat milk, 1/2 cup cooked green beans, and 3/4 cup 4.5% fat cottage cheese.

This recipe courtesy of the California Pistachio Commission (www.pistachios.org).

Peking Pork Pasta Salad

Serving Size: 1/6 recipe, **Total Servings:** 6

1 tsp vegetable oil
1 lb pork tenderloin, cut into 1/4-inch thick slices
1/2 cup light soy sauce
1/2 cup dry sherry
1 tsp sesame oil
8 oz corkscrew pasta, cooked and drained, room temperature
1 cup sliced green onion, including some green tops
1/2 cup diced green pepper
1/4 cup toasted almond slices
8 oz fresh spinach leaves, washed and drained

1. In a nonstick frying pan, heat vegetable oil over medium-high heat. Add pork and stir-fry quickly. Remove pork from pan and place in a large bowl.

2. Combine light soy sauce, sherry, and sesame oil. Pour half over the pork strips and toss well. Toss pasta together with green onion, green pepper, and almonds.

3. Arrange pasta mixture on spinach leaves, top with pork, and serve remaining soy sauce mixture on the side.

EXCHANGES

2 Starch	2 Lean Meat	1 Vegetable

Calories	314
Calories from Fat	62
Total Fat	7 g
Saturated Fat	1.3 g
Polyunsaturated Fat	1.5 g
Monounsaturated Fat	3.1 g
Cholesterol	44 mg
Sodium	840 mg
Total Carbohydrate	34 g
Dietary Fiber	3 g
Sugars	4 g
Protein	25 g

FITTING YOUR PLAN

CALORIE PLAN	
1500	1 serving Peking Pork Pasta Salad, 1/2 cup canned plums in extra-light syrup, 8 oz nonfat milk, and 1/2 cup coleslaw made with 1 cup cabbage and carrots combined, mixed with a little vinegar and 2 Tbsp reduced-fat mayonnaise.
1800	(give 1 lean-meat exchange to another meal): 1 serving Peking Pork Pasta Salad, 1/2 cup canned plums in extra-light syrup, 8 oz nonfat milk, and 1/2 cup coleslaw made with 1 cup cabbage and carrots combined, mixed with a little vinegar and 2 Tbsp reduced-fat mayonnaise.
2000	(give 1 lean-meat exchange to another meal): 1 serving Peking Pork Pasta Salad, 1/2 cup canned plums in extra-light syrup, 8 oz nonfat milk, and 1/2 cup coleslaw made with 1 cup cabbage and carrots combined, mixed with a little vinegar and 2 Tbsp reduced-fat mayonnaise.

This recipe courtesy of the National Pork Board (www.porkandhealth.org).

Pomegranate Shrimp Sauté

Serving Size: 1/5 recipe, **Total Servings:** 5

2 Tbsp toasted sesame oil
2 Tbsp vegetable oil
2 Tbsp whole coriander seeds
2 Tbsp ground cumin
   Freshly ground black pepper
1 Tbsp black mustard seeds
30 large shrimp (1 1/4 lb), peeled
   and deveined
1/2 cup pomegranate juice★
1 Tbsp red wine vinegar
1 tsp kosher salt
1/2 lb light-colored frisee (chicory),
   heavy stems removed, leaf
   portion torn into 2-inch
   pieces (2 packed cups)
   Seeds from 1/4 large or
   1/2 small pomegranate
   (about 2 Tbsp)

★To make 1 cup of pomegranate juice, put
1 1/2 to 2 cups of seeds in a blender; blend until
liquefied. Pour mixture through a cheesecloth-
lined strainer or sieve.

1. In a 12-inch skillet, combine
1 Tbsp sesame oil with vegetable oil,
coriander seeds, cumin, pepper, and
black mustard seeds. Place over
medium heat and cook, stirring for
4 minutes.

2. Raise heat. Stir in the shrimp
and cook, turning and stirring, for
3 minutes or until shrimp are opaque.

3. Reduce heat. Stir in the pomegranate juice, vinegar, and salt. Cook,
stirring and scraping bottom of pan,
for 1 minute. Stir in remaining sesame
oil.

4. Place 1/2 cup frisee on each plate.
Top with shrimp and drizzle sauce
around plate. Sprinkle with pomegranate seeds.

EXCHANGES

1/2 Fruit	2 Very Lean Meat
1 Vegetable	2 1/2 Fat

Calories 230
    Calories from Fat 121
Total Fat . . . . 13 g
    Saturated Fat . . . . 1.5 g
    Polyunsaturated Fat . . . . 4.6 g
    Monounsaturated Fat . . . . 6.6 g
Cholesterol . . . . 131 mg
Sodium . . . . 640 mg
Total Carbohydrate . . . . 12 g
    Dietary Fiber . . . . 4 g
    Sugars . . . . 5 g
Protein . . . . 17 g

FITTING YOUR PLAN

This recipe uses very lean meat instead of lean meat, so the difference for fat per serving is 4–6 g (approximately 1 fat exchange), which can be added to this meal.

CALORIE PLAN

1500   1 serving Pomegranate Shrimp Sauté, 2/3 cup couscous, 1 small tangerine, 8 oz nonfat milk, 1/2 cup Italian beans, and 1 1/2 tsp low-fat margarine.

1800   (save 1 lean-meat exchange for another meal): 1 serving Pomegranate Shrimp Sauté, 2/3 cup couscous, 1 small tangerine, 8 oz nonfat milk, 1/2 cup Italian beans, and 1 1/2 tsp low-fat margarine.

2000   (save 1 lean-meat exchange for another meal): 1 serving Pomegranate Shrimp Sauté, 2/3 cup couscous, 1 small tangerine, 8 oz nonfat milk, 1/2 cup Italian beans, and 1 1/2 tsp low-fat margarine.

This recipe courtesy of the Pomegranate Council (www.pomegranates.org).

Red Cabbage

Serving Size: 1/10 recipe, **Total Servings:** 10

2–3 lb red cabbage
1/4 lb extra-lean turkey bacon
  1 medium onion
   Vegetable oil
1/2 cup raisins
2–3 bay leaves
6–8 juniper berries (*optional*)
1–4 whole cloves
1/2 cup red wine
2–6 Tbsp sugar
  1 medium apple
   Salt and pepper
  2 Tbsp flour

1. Wash and coarsely shred the cabbage. Coarsely dice the bacon and the peeled onion. Sauté in a large pot the bacon and onion. Add a little vegetable oil as necessary. After the diced onion is light golden in color, add large handfuls of the shredded cabbage. Stir as the cabbage glazes (be careful to not let it burn). When all of the cabbage has been added and is glazed (about half the volume of the starting amount of the cabbage), add raisins, bay leaves, juniper berries, cloves, wine, sugar, and enough water to cover. Peel and shred the apple and add into pot.

2. Simmer until tender (1–2 hours). Add salt and pepper to taste. Add additional sugar and wine to taste. Mix flour with a little cold water and add to thicken.

EXCHANGES

1 Fruit	1/2 Fat	1 Vegetable

Calories	94
Calories from Fat	12
Total Fat	1 g
Saturated Fat	0.4 g
Polyunsaturated Fat	0.3 g
Monounsaturated Fat	0.1 g
Cholesterol	4 mg
Sodium	76 mg
Total Carbohydrate	20 g
Dietary Fiber	3 g
Sugars	15 g
Protein	3 g

FITTING YOUR PLAN

CALORIE PLAN

1500 1 serving Red Cabbage, 1/2 cup boiled potatoes, 1 small (1 oz) dinner roll, 8 oz nonfat milk, 1 cup salad made from nonstarchy vegetables, 1 tsp olive oil on salad with vinegar to taste, 1 1/2 tsp low-fat margarine, and 2 oz lean fish, chicken, or beef.

1800 1 serving Red Cabbage, 1/2 cup boiled potatoes, 1 small (1 oz) dinner roll, 8 oz nonfat milk, 1 cup salad made from nonstarchy vegetables, 1 tsp olive oil on salad with vinegar to taste, 1 1/2 tsp low-fat margarine, and 3 oz lean fish, chicken, or beef.

2000 1 serving Red Cabbage, 1/2 cup boiled potatoes, 1 small (1 oz) dinner roll, 8 oz nonfat milk, 1 cup salad made from nonstarchy vegetables, 1 tsp olive oil on salad with vinegar to taste, 1 1/2 tsp low-fat margarine, and 3 oz lean fish, chicken, or beef.

This recipe courtesy of the Leafy Greens Council (www.leafy-greens.org).

Red Pepper Mango Onion Sauce

Serving Size: 1/6 recipe, **Total Servings:** 6

1 1/4 cups chopped onion
   1 cup chopped red bell pepper
   1 Tbsp olive oil
   1 Tbsp flour
3/4 cup fresh mango fruit, peeled
      and cubed
   1 cup bottled or canned mango
      nectar
   1 Tbsp minced ginger root
   2 tsp balsamic vinegar or white
      wine vinegar
1/4 teaspoon crushed red pepper
      flakes

1. Sauté onions, bell pepper, and oil in a skillet over medium heat for 5–8 minutes or until tender. Stir in flour; then add mango, mango nectar, ginger, vinegar, and red pepper. Cook, stirring over medium heat until sauce boils and is thickened. Serve hot with barbecued or broiled chicken, fish, sausage, or pork.

EXCHANGES
1 Fruit   1/2 Fat

Calories	84
Calories from Fat	23
Total Fat	3 g
Saturated Fat	0.3 g
Polyunsaturated Fat	0.3 g
Monounsaturated Fat	1.7 g
Cholesterol	0 mg
Sodium	3 mg
Total Carbohydrate	16 g
Dietary Fiber	2 g
Sugars	13 g
Protein	1 g

FITTING YOUR PLAN

CALORIE PLAN	
1500	1 serving Red Pepper Mango Onion Sauce, 2/3 cup pasta or rice, 8 oz nonfat milk, 1 cup cooked spinach, 1 1/2 tsp margarine, and 2 oz lean chicken, fish, or pork.
1800	1 serving Red Pepper Mango Onion Sauce, 2/3 cup pasta or rice, 8 oz nonfat milk, 1 cup cooked spinach, 1 1/2 tsp margarine, and 3 oz lean chicken, fish, or pork.
2000	1 serving Red Pepper Mango Onion Sauce, 2/3 cup pasta or rice, 8 oz nonfat milk, 1 cup cooked spinach, 1 1/2 tsp margarine, and 3 oz lean chicken, fish, or pork.

This recipe courtesy of the National Onion Association (NOA) (www.onions-usa.org).

Savory Fruit Sausage Sauté

Serving Size: 1/6 recipe, **Total Servings:** 6

1/3 cup apple juice
1 Tbsp Dijon-style mustard
1 Tbsp cider vinegar
1 tsp vegetable oil
1 lb turkey kielbasa sausage, sliced 1/3 inch thick
1 cup sliced onion
2 medium tart red apples, cored and sliced 1/3 inch thick
1 cup (about 6 oz) pitted dried plums, halved
Salt and pepper

1. In a small bowl, whisk apple juice, mustard, and vinegar; set aside. In a large skillet, heat oil over medium-high heat. Add sausage and onion; cook and stir 5 minutes. Add apples; cook and stir 5 minutes. Add dried plums and apple juice mixture; reduce heat to low. Cover and cook 10 minutes, stirring occasionally. Season to taste with salt and pepper. Serve immediately.

EXCHANGES

2 Fruit	1/2 Fat	2 Lean Meat

Calories 232	
Calories from Fat 82	
Total Fat . . . . 9 g	
Saturated Fat . . . . 2.1 g	
Polyunsaturated Fat . . . . 3.0 g	
Monounsaturated Fat . . . . 3.3 g	
Cholesterol . . . . 60 mg	
Sodium. . . . . 768 mg	
Total Carbohydrate . . . . 30 g	
Dietary Fiber. . . . . 4 g	
Sugars . . . . 21 g	
Protein . . . . 13 g	

FITTING YOUR PLAN

CALORIE PLAN	
1500	(borrow 1 fruit exchange from breakfast): 1 serving Savory Fruit Sausage Sauté, 2/3 cup brown rice, 8 oz nonfat milk, 1 cup steamed broccoli, and 1 1/2 tsp margarine.
1800	(borrow 1 fruit exchange from snack and give 1 lean-meat exchange to another meal or snack): 1 serving Savory Fruit Sausage Sauté, 2/3 cup brown rice, 8 oz nonfat milk, 1 cup steamed broccoli, and 1 1/2 tsp margarine.
2000	(borrow 1 fruit exchange from snack and give 1 lean-meat exchange to another meal or snack): 1 serving Savory Fruit Sausage Sauté, 2/3 cup brown rice, 8 oz nonfat milk, 1 cup steamed broccoli, and 1 1/2 tsp margarine.

This recipe courtesy of the California Dried Plum Board (www.californiadriedplums.org).

Seven-Layer Salad

Serving Size: 1/8 recipe, **Total Servings:** 8

DRESSING
1/2 cup fat-free mayonnaise
3/4 cup fat-free sour cream or yogurt
1/4 cup Florida parsley, chopped
1/2 tsp cayenne pepper
2 tsp Worcestershire sauce
1 tsp Florida garlic, chopped fine
2 tsp Florida sugar

SALAD
3 cups Florida cabbage, shredded (about half of a head)
2 cups Florida broccoli stems, grated
2 cups Florida carrots, grated
1 cup Florida celery, grated
2 cups Florida cauliflower, cut small
1/4 cup bacon, cooked (approximately 6 oz raw)

1. Combine all of the ingredients for the dressing. In a glass bowl, layer cabbage and broccoli; then spread a third of the dressing over layered vegetables.

2. Continue to layer carrot, celery, and cauliflower. Spread remaining dressing over cauliflower and refrigerate at least 2 hours, preferably overnight. Sprinkle with bacon and serve.

EXCHANGES

1/2 Carbohydrate	2 Vegetable

Calories 90	
Calories from Fat 19	
Total Fat . . . . 2 g	
Saturated Fat . . . . 0.7 g	
Polyunsaturated Fat . . . . 0.5 g	
Monounsaturated Fat . . . . 0.2 g	
Cholesterol . . . . 9 mg	
Sodium . . . . 318 mg	
Total Carbohydrate . . . . 14 g	
Dietary Fiber . . . . 3 g	
Sugars . . . . 7 g	
Protein . . . . 4 g	

FITTING YOUR PLAN

For this meal plan, the 1/2 carbohydrate exchange is calculated as 1/2 starch exchange.

CALORIE PLAN

1500 1 serving Seven-Layer Salad, 1 1/2 oz pumpernickel bread, 1 cup mixed raspberries and honeydew melon, 1 Tbsp reduced-fat margarine, 8 oz nonfat milk, 10 peanuts, and 2 oz lean baked chicken, fish, pork, or beef.

1800 1 serving Seven-Layer Salad, 1 1/2 oz pumpernickel bread, 1 cup mixed raspberries and honeydew melon, 1 Tbsp reduced-fat margarine, 8 oz nonfat milk, 10 peanuts, and 3 oz lean baked chicken, fish, pork, or beef.

2000 1 serving Seven-Layer Salad, 1 1/2 oz pumpernickel bread, 1 cup mixed raspberries and honeydew melon, 1 Tbsp reduced-fat margarine, 8 oz nonfat milk, 10 peanuts, and 3 oz lean baked chicken, fish, pork, or beef.

This recipe courtesy of the Florida Department of Agriculture (www.florida-agriculture.com).

Soup Fresh from the Garden

Serving Size: 1/6 recipe, **Total Servings:** 6

2 cups sweet potatoes, cubed
3/4 cup sliced yellow squash
3/4 cup zucchini slices, quartered
1/2 cup green beans, cut up
1/2 cup whole-kernel corn
1 medium onion, chopped
1 small clove garlic, minced
1/2 tsp chili seasoning
5 1/2 cups reduced-sodium, fat-free vegetable broth
1 can (14 1/2 oz) chopped tomatoes
1/4 cup green onions, sliced
2 Tbsp parsley, chopped
4 oz shredded 75% reduced-fat light cheddar cheese, shredded

1. In a 4-quart saucepan, combine the first 10 ingredients. Bring to a boil, reduce heat, and simmer 15 minutes or until vegetables are tender. Add green onions and parsley; cook 5 minutes longer. To serve, garnish each serving with cheese.

EXCHANGES

1 Starch	1/2 Fat	2 Vegetable

Calories	145
Calories from Fat	18
Total Fat	2 g
Saturated Fat	1.0 g
Polyunsaturated Fat	0.2 g
Monounsaturated Fat	0.4 g
Cholesterol	7 mg
Sodium	610 mg
Total Carbohydrate	24 g
Dietary Fiber	4 g
Sugars	10 g
Protein	9 g

FITTING YOUR PLAN

CALORIE PLAN	
1500	1 serving Soup Fresh from the Garden, 1 biscuit (2 1/2 inches across), 1/2 cup canned pears in juice with 6 oz fat-free plain yogurt, 2 oz lean meat or cheese, and 5 peanuts.
1800	1 serving Soup Fresh from the Garden, 1 biscuit (2 1/2 inches across), 1/2 cup canned pears in juice with 6 oz fat-free plain yogurt, 3 oz lean meat or cheese, and 5 peanuts.
2000	1 serving Soup Fresh from the Garden, 1 biscuit (2 1/2 inches across), 1/2 cup canned pears in juice with 6 oz fat-free plain yogurt, 3 oz lean meat or cheese, and 5 peanuts.

This recipe courtesy of the North Carolina Sweetpotato Commission (www.ncsweetpotatoes.com).

Southwestern Pork and Bean Salad

Serving Size: 1/3 recipe, **Total Servings:** 3

SALAD

1 can (14 oz) red kidney beans, rinsed and drained
1 can (7 oz) corn kernels, drained
1 small carrot, chopped
1/2 red pepper, chopped
1/2 cup sliced celery
2 green onions, chopped
1 tsp dried parsley
1 cup cubed, cooked pork

DRESSING

1/4 cup red wine vinegar
1 Tbsp canola oil
1 clove garlic, minced
1/4 tsp salt
Pinch freshly ground black pepper
Dash hot pepper sauce

1. In a serving bowl, gently toss salad ingredients together.

2. In a separate small bowl, whisk together dressing ingredients. Pour over salad and toss gently to combine. Chill for 30–60 minutes, occasionally stirring lightly.

EXCHANGES

2 Starch	2 Lean Meat	1 Vegetable

Calories	275
Calories from Fat	66
Total Fat	7 g
Saturated Fat	1.0 g
Polyunsaturated Fat	2.0 g
Monounsaturated Fat	3.6 g
Cholesterol	30 mg
Sodium	488 mg
Total Carbohydrate	35 g
Dietary Fiber	8 g
Sugars	7 g
Protein	20 g

FITTING YOUR PLAN

CALORIE PLAN	
1500	1 serving Southwestern Pork and Bean Salad, 8 oz nonfat milk, 1/2 cup cooked kale, 1/2 cup unsweetened applesauce, 6 almonds, and 1 tsp tub margarine.
1800	(save 1 lean-meat exchange for another meal): 1 serving Southwestern Pork and Bean Salad, 8 oz nonfat milk, 1/2 cup cooked kale, 1/2 cup unsweetened applesauce, 6 almonds, and 1 tsp tub margarine.
2000	(save 1 lean-meat exchange for another meal): 1 serving Southwestern Pork and Bean Salad, 8 oz nonfat milk, 1/2 cup cooked kale, 1/2 cup unsweetened applesauce, 6 almonds, and 1 tsp tub margarine.

This recipe courtesy of the Canola Council of Canada (www.canola-council.org).

Spicy Mint Chicken

Serving Size: 1/2 cup, **Total Servings:** 6

1/4 cup cracked wheat cereal
1/2 cup boiling water
2 large red tomatoes (or 7–8 oz diced canned tomatoes)
1/4 cup chopped fresh mint leaves
1 Tbsp vegetable oil
1 cinnamon stick
2 small bay leaves
1 1/2 cups chopped onion
4 cloves garlic, minced
1 lb skinless, boneless chicken breasts, diced
1/8 tsp ginger
1/8 tsp black pepper
1/8 tsp cayenne pepper (*optional*)
1/2 tsp salt
1/16 tsp cinnamon
1/16 tsp nutmeg
1/16 tsp mace
1/16 tsp cloves

1. Soak cracked wheat in boiling water; set aside. In a blender, puree tomatoes and mint leaves; set aside.

2. In a large saucepan, heat oil over medium-high heat. Add cinnamon stick, bay leaves, onion, and garlic; sauté until onion is clear.

3. Add chicken, ginger, black pepper, cayenne pepper, and salt; cook over medium-high heat for 8 minutes.

4. Add undrained cracked wheat and tomato-mint puree. Cook until meat is done and gravy is thickened, about 8–10 minutes, stirring often.

5. Sprinkle cinnamon, nutmeg, mace, and cloves over meat mixture and mix well. Serve hot with chapati, an unleavened pancake-like bread from India.

EXCHANGES

1/2 Starch	2 Very Lean Meat
1 Vegetable	1/2 Fat

Calories 166
  Calories from Fat 42
Total Fat . . . . 5 g
  Saturated Fat . . . . 0.7 g
  Polyunsaturated Fat. . . . . 1.3 g
  Monounsaturated Fat . . . . 2.1 g
Cholesterol . . . . 46 mg
Sodium. . . . . 241 mg
Total Carbohydrate . . . . 12 g
  Dietary Fiber. 2 g
  Sugars . . . . 5 g
Protein . . . . 19 g

FITTING YOUR PLAN

This recipe was calculated for very-lean-meat exchanges, which have 0–1 g of fat per ounce. With 2 very-lean-meat exchanges, you can have an extra 4–6 g of fat (approximately 1 fat exchange) using this meal pattern.

CALORIE PLAN

1500   1 serving Spicy Mint Chicken, 1 1/2 oz chapati bread, 1/2 large fresh pear, 8 oz nonfat milk, 1 cup salad made from nonstarchy vegetables, and 2 1/2 Tbsp salad dressing.

1800   (give 1 lean-meat exchange to another meal or have 1 oz low-fat cheese): 1 serving Spicy Mint Chicken, 1 1/2 oz chapati bread, 1/2 large fresh pear, 8 oz nonfat milk, 1 cup salad made from nonstarchy vegetables, and 2 1/2 Tbsp salad dressing.

2000   (give 1 lean-meat exchange to another meal or use 1 oz low-fat cheese): 1 serving Spicy Mint Chicken, 1 1/2 oz chapati bread, 1/2 large fresh pear, 8 oz nonfat milk, 1 cup salad made from nonstarchy vegetables, and 2 1/2 Tbsp salad dressing.

This recipe courtesy of the Kansas Wheat Commission (www.kswheat.com).

Stewed Catfish★

Serving Size: 1/6 recipe, **Total Servings:** 6

1 1/2 lb skinless, boneless Florida
catfish fillets

2 slices turkey bacon, cut into
thirds

1 cup chopped onions

1 can (28 oz) tomatoes

1 can (16 oz) peas and carrots,
drained

1 cup chili sauce

2 Tbsp Worcestershire sauce

1/2 tsp pepper

★This recipe is high in sodium. Adjust the rest of
your meals over the day to compensate for this.

1. Cut fillets into 1-inch pieces; set
aside. Place bacon in a 3-quart
microwave-safe dish. Cover and cook
in microwave on high for 3 minutes.
Add onions and cook an additional
2 minutes. Add remaining ingredients,
except fish. Cook for 5 minutes; then
stir. Cook 5 additional minutes. Add
fish and cook for 10 minutes or until
fish flakes easily when tested with a
fork.

EXCHANGES

1/2 Starch	3 Lean Meat	3 Vegetable

Calories	280
Calories from Fat	77
Total Fat	9 g
Saturated Fat	2.8 g
Polyunsaturated Fat	1.6 g
Monounsaturated Fat	3.8 g
Cholesterol	64 mg
Sodium	1035 mg
Total Carbohydrate	25 g
Dietary Fiber	5 g
Sugars	12 g
Protein	26 g

FITTING YOUR PLAN

CALORIE PLAN

1500 (borrow 1 vegetable exchange from a snack and 1 lean-meat exchange from breakfast):
1 serving Stewed Catfish, 3-inch cube of corn bread (3 oz), 17 small grapes, and 1 1/2 tsp
low-fat margarine.

1800 (borrow 1 vegetable exchange from a snack): 1 serving Stewed Catfish, 3-inch cube of corn
bread (3 oz), 17 small grapes, 8 oz nonfat milk, and 1 1/2 tsp low-fat margarine.

2000 (borrow 1 vegetable exchange from a snack): 1 serving Stewed Catfish, 3-inch cube of corn
bread (3 oz), 17 small grapes, 8 oz nonfat milk, and 1 1/2 tsp low-fat margarine.

This recipe courtesy of the Florida Department of Agriculture (www.florida-agriculture.com).

Technicolor Vegetable Sauté

Serving Size: 1/4 recipe, **Total Servings:** 4

2 tsp olive oil
1 cup baby carrots (2-inch pieces), scrubbed
1 1/3 cups pattypan squash (also called summer squash), ends removed and cut into wedges
1 2/3 cups green beans, cut to 2 1/2 inches and blanched
1 cup California ripe olives, whole
1 1/2 tsp thyme, chopped
1 tsp garlic, minced
1/2 tsp salt
1 tsp unsalted butter
2/3 cup red beets, steamed, peeled and diced into 1-inch pieces

1. Heat oil in a large sauté pan over medium heat. Add carrots and cook for 4–5 minutes, stirring occasionally until lightly browned. Add squash and continue to cook for 3–4 minutes, until tender. Stir in green beans, olives, thyme, garlic, and salt and cook for 2–3 minutes until heated through. Toss with butter and sprinkle with beets.

EXCHANGES

3 Vegetable   1 Fat

Calories	120
Calories from Fat	65
Total Fat	7 g
Saturated Fat	1.4 g
Polyunsaturated Fat	0.7 g
Monounsaturated Fat	4.6 g
Cholesterol	3 mg
Sodium	631 mg
Total Carbohydrate	14 g
Dietary Fiber	5 g
Sugars	5 g
Protein	3 g

FITTING YOUR PLAN

CALORIE PLAN

1500 (borrow 1 vegetable exchange from another meal or snack): 1 serving Technicolor Vegetable Sauté, 1/2 cup sweet potato, 1 small (1 oz) whole-grain dinner roll, 3/4 cup fresh pineapple, 8 oz nonfat milk, 2 oz baked lean chicken, and 1 Tbsp low-fat margarine.

1800 (borrow 1 vegetable exchange from another meal or snack): 1 serving Technicolor Vegetable Sauté, 1/2 cup sweet potato, 1 small (1 oz) whole-grain dinner roll, 3/4 cup fresh pineapple, 8 oz nonfat milk, 3 oz baked lean chicken, and 1 Tbsp low-fat margarine.

2000 (borrow 1 vegetable exchange from another meal or snack): 1 serving Technicolor Vegetable Sauté, 1/2 cup sweet potato, 1 small (1 oz) whole-grain dinner roll, 3/4 cup fresh pineapple, 8 oz nonfat milk, 3 oz baked lean chicken, and 1 Tbsp low-fat margarine.

This recipe courtesy of the California Olive Industry (www.californiaolives.org).

Three-Grain Pilaf

Serving Size: 1/2 cup, **Total Servings:** 14

1 Tbsp vegetable oil
1 cup dry bulgur
1/2 cup dry white long-grain rice★
1/2 cup dry pearled barley
2 bouillon cubes or 2 Tbsp bouillon granules
4 cups hot water
1/2 cup coarsely grated carrots
1/2 cup chopped onions
1/2 cup sliced almonds, toasted (*optional*)

★Do not substitute minute or brown rice.

1. Add oil to wok or skillet and heat on medium high. Add grains and sauté for 7 minutes, stirring occasionally.

2. Dissolve bouillon in hot water and stir into grains; add vegetables. Cover, reduce heat, and simmer 25–30 minutes. Stir occasionally until liquid is absorbed and grains are tender.

3. Remove from heat, let stand 5 minutes, and fluff with fork. Garnish with almonds, if desired. Makes 7 cups.

Variations

Season with black pepper or herbs. Add other vegetables such as chopped green pepper, red pepper, celery, peas, or broccoli.

EXCHANGES
1 Starch

Calories 90
   Calories from Fat 11
Total Fat . . . . 1 g
   Saturated Fat . . . . 0.1 g
   Polyunsaturated Fat . . . . 0.4 g
   Monounsaturated Fat . . . . 0.6 g
Cholesterol . . . . 0 mg
Sodium . . . . 134 mg
Total Carbohydrate . . . . 18 g
   Dietary Fiber . . . . 3 g
   Sugars . . . . 1 g
Protein . . . . 2 g

FITTING YOUR PLAN

CALORIE PLAN	
1500	2 servings Three-Grain Pilaf, 1 cup cooked chopped red and green peppers and broccoli, 1 small orange, 8 oz nonfat milk, 2 oz lean grilled chicken, and 12 almonds.
1800	2 servings Three-Grain Pilaf, 1 cup cooked chopped red and green peppers and broccoli, 1 small orange, 8 oz nonfat milk, 3 oz lean grilled chicken, and 12 almonds.
2000	2 servings Three-Grain Pilaf, 1 cup cooked chopped red and green peppers and broccoli, 1 small orange, 8 oz nonfat milk, 3 oz lean grilled chicken, and 12 almonds.

This recipe courtesy of the Kansas Wheat Commission (www.kswheat.com).

Tomato Garbanzo Salad

Serving Size: 1/8 recipe, **Total Servings:** 8

3 cups (about 1 1/2 lb) diced, fresh California tomatoes

1 cup chopped red onion

1/4 cup chopped parsley

1 1/2 Tbsp lemon juice

1 tsp finely chopped garlic

1/2 tsp dill

1/2 tsp red pepper flakes

1 tsp salt

1/4 tsp pepper

1/3 cup canola oil

3 cups (two 15-1/4 oz cans) garbanzo beans, drained

2 hard-cooked eggs, finely chopped

1. Combine California tomatoes and the next eight ingredients. Stir in canola oil. Fold in beans and hard-cooked eggs.

EXCHANGES

1 Starch	2 Fat	2 Vegetable

Calories	221
Calories from Fat	110
Total Fat	12 g
Saturated Fat	1.2 g
Polyunsaturated Fat	3.7 g
Monounsaturated Fat	6.4 g
Cholesterol	53 mg
Sodium	417 mg
Total Carbohydrate	22 g
Dietary Fiber	6 g
Sugars	6 g
Protein	8 g

FITTING YOUR PLAN

CALORIE PLAN	
1500	1 serving Tomato Garbanzo Salad, 1/2 cup green peas, 1/2 cup unsweetened applesauce, 8 oz nonfat milk, and 2 oz lean chicken or fish.
1800	1 serving Tomato Garbanzo Salad, 1/2 cup green peas, 1/2 cup unsweetened applesauce, 8 oz nonfat milk, and 3 oz lean chicken or fish.
2000	1 serving Tomato Garbanzo Salad, 1/2 cup green peas, 1/2 cup unsweetened applesauce, 8 oz nonfat milk, and 3 oz lean chicken or fish.

This recipe courtesy of the California Tomato Commission (www.tomato.org).

Turkey Moussaka

Serving Size: 1/6 recipe, **Total Servings:** 6

Olive oil cooking spray
2 1/2 lb eggplant, cut into
1/4-inch slices
1 lb ground turkey
1/2 cup onion, chopped
2 cloves garlic, minced
3/4 cup white wine
1 can (8 oz) tomato sauce
1 Tbsp Italian seasoning, crushed
1/2 tsp pepper
1/4 tsp salt
1/8 tsp nutmeg
1/4 cup flour
1 can (12 oz) evaporated nonfat milk
1/2 cup low-sodium chicken broth
1/4 cup grated Parmesan cheese

1. Coat two (15 X 10 X 1-inch) baking sheets with cooking spray. Arrange eggplant slices in a single layer on baking sheets; lightly coat top of eggplant slices with cooking spray. Bake in 425°F oven for 15 minutes or until lightly browned. Set aside.

2. In a large nonstick skillet, over medium heat, sauté turkey, onions, and garlic for 5–6 minutes or until turkey is no longer pink. Drain meat juices from skillet. Return skillet to heat; add wine, tomato sauce, Italian seasoning, 1/4 tsp pepper, salt, and nutmeg. Cook 8–10 minutes or until most of the liquid is evaporated. Remove from heat.

3. In a medium saucepan combine the flour and remaining 1/4 tsp pepper. With a wire whisk, slowly add evaporated milk and broth. Cook mixture over medium heat, stirring constantly with whisk, until sauce begins to bubble and thickens. Remove pan from heat. With wire whisk, fold in Parmesan cheese.

4. In the bottom of a 13 X 9 X 2-inch baking pan, arrange a third of the eggplant slices. Top with a third of the turkey mixture and a third of the white sauce. Repeat layers with remaining ingredients. Bake in 350°F oven for 30 minutes or until heated throughout.

EXCHANGES

1/2 Carbohydrate	3 Lean Meat
3 Vegetable	

Calories 281
    Calories from Fat 83
Total Fat . . . . 9 g
    Saturated Fat . . . . 2.7 g
    Polyunsaturated Fat. . . . . 2.1 g
    Monounsaturated Fat . . . . 3.2 g
Cholesterol . . . . 62 mg
Sodium. . . . . 501 mg
Total Carbohydrate . . . . 26 g
    Dietary Fiber. 5 g
    Sugars . . . . 16 g
Protein . . . . 24 g

FITTING YOUR PLAN

CALORIE PLAN

1500 (borrow 1 vegetable and 1 lean-meat exchange from another meal or snack): 1 serving Turkey Moussaka, 1 slice 120-calorie whole-grain bread or 1 1/2 oz bread, 8 oz nonfat milk, 1 cup mixed cantaloupe and honeydew melon pieces, and 12 mixed nuts.

1800 (borrow 1 vegetable exchange from another meal or snack): 1 serving Turkey Moussaka, 1 slice 120-calorie whole-grain bread or 1 1/2 oz bread, 8 oz nonfat milk, 1 cup mixed cantaloupe and honeydew melon pieces, and 12 mixed nuts.

2000 (borrow 1 vegetable exchange from another meal or snack): 1 serving Turkey Moussaka, 1 slice 120-calorie whole-grain bread or 1 1/2 oz bread, 8 oz nonfat milk, 1 cup mixed cantaloupe and honeydew melon pieces, and 12 mixed nuts.

This recipe courtesy of the National Turkey Federation (www.eatturkey.com).

Turkey, Rotini, and Split Pea Salad

Serving Size: 1/5 recipe, **Total Servings:** 5

2 cups rotini, uncooked
1 cup USA split peas, rinsed
3 1/2 oz cooked turkey, diced
1/4 cup green pepper, diced
1/2 cup carrot, grated
2 Tbsp sliced black olives
2 Tbsp green onion, sliced
2 Tbsp grated Parmesan cheese
1/4 cup fresh parsley, snipped

DRESSING

8 oz nonfat yogurt
2 cloves garlic, minced
1 1/2 Tbsp olive oil
2 Tbsp tarragon white vinegar
3/4 tsp dry mustard
1/2 tsp crushed oregano
1/2 tsp crushed basil
1/4 tsp crushed red pepper
1/4 tsp salt

1. Cook rotini according to package directions. Drain, rinse, and cool. Add split peas to 2 cups boiling water. Reduce heat, cover, and simmer for 20 minutes. Drain and cool. Combine cooked rotini and split peas with other ingredients. Meanwhile, combine all dressing ingredients together and toss with salad. Chill several hours before serving.

EXCHANGES

3 Starch	1 Lean Meat
1 Vegetable	1/2 Fat

Calories	349
Calories from Fat	65
Total Fat	7 g
Saturated Fat	1.5 g
Polyunsaturated Fat	1.0 g
Monounsaturated Fat	3.8 g
Cholesterol	18 mg
Sodium	241 mg
Total Carbohydrate	50 g
Dietary Fiber	10 g
Sugars	8 g
Protein	22 g

FITTING YOUR PLAN

CALORIE PLAN

1500 (borrow 1 starch exchange from a snack): 1 serving Turkey, Rotini, and Split Pea Salad, 1/2 cup canned pears in extra-light syrup mixed with 6 oz fat-free plain yogurt, 1 cup raw mixed cucumber slices and tomato, 1 oz cheese (3 g of fat or less per ounce), and 3 Tbsp reduced-fat salad dressing on vegetables.

1800 (borrow 1 starch exchange from a snack): 1 serving Turkey, Rotini, and Split Pea Salad, 1/2 cup canned pears in extra-light syrup mixed with 6 oz fat-free plain yogurt, 1 cup raw mixed cucumber slices and tomato, 2 oz cheese (3 g of fat or less per ounce), and 3 Tbsp reduced-fat salad dressing on vegetables.

2000 (borrow 1 starch exchange from a snack): 1 serving Turkey, Rotini, and Split Pea Salad, 1/2 cup canned pears in extra-light syrup mixed with 6 oz fat-free plain yogurt, 1 cup raw mixed cucumber slices and tomato, 2 oz cheese (3 g of fat or less per ounce), and 3 Tbsp reduced-fat salad dressing on vegetables.

This recipe courtesy of the U.S.A. Dry Pea & Lentil Council (www.pea-lentil.com).

Zydeco Gumbo

Serving Size: 1/8 recipe, **Total Servings:** 8

1 1/4 lb boneless chicken, cubed
   2 medium onions, cut into wedges
   1 green pepper, cut into narrow strips
   1 can (1 lb, 13 oz) whole tomatoes
 1/4 cup Worcestershire sauce
   2 Tbsp prepared mustard
   2 Tbsp minced garlic
   1 tsp thyme
   1 tsp rosemary
 1/2 tsp black pepper
 1/2 lb shrimp meat
   3 cups hot cooked rice

1. Combine all ingredients, except the shrimp and rice, in a large saucepan. Cover and bring to a boil. Simmer 45 minutes or until chicken is tender and flavors blend together. Add shrimp and heat 1 minute. Serve with scoops of rice in wide soup bowls.

EXCHANGES

1 Starch	2 Lean Meat	2 Vegetable

Calories 241
   Calories from Fat 39
Total Fat . . . . 4 g
   Saturated Fat . . . . 1.1 g
   Polyunsaturated Fat. . . . . 1.1 g
   Monounsaturated Fat . . . . 1.5 g
Cholesterol . . . . 83 mg
Sodium. . . . . 383 mg
Total Carbohydrate . . . . 28 g
   Dietary Fiber. 3 g
   Sugars . . . . 8 g
Protein . . . . 22 g

FITTING YOUR PLAN

CALORIE PLAN

1500   1 serving Zydeco Gumbo, 1 slice (1 oz) rye bread, 1/2 cup canned peaches in extra-light syrup, 8 oz nonfat milk, 1 tsp margarine, and 4 pecan halves.

1800   (save 1 lean-meat exchange for another meal or snack): 1 serving Zydeco Gumbo, 1 slice reduced-calorie bread, 1/2 cup canned peaches in extra-light syrup, 8 oz nonfat milk, 1 tsp margarine, and 4 pecan halves.

2000   (save 1 lean-meat exchange for another meal or snack): 1 serving Zydeco Gumbo, 1 slice reduced-calorie bread, 1/2 cup canned peaches in extra-light syrup, 8 oz nonfat milk, 1 tsp margarine, and 4 pecan halves.

This recipe courtesy of the National Onion Association (NOA) (www.onions–usa.org).

Snacks

A Note about Snacks

If you are following one of the meal plans from this book, here is a list of possible snacks.

1500 Calorie Plan

The 1500 calorie plan includes 1 starch, 1 vegetable, and 1 fat exchange for the midafternoon snack. You can eat these foods at different times during the afternoon. Possible suggestions are

1. one slice of unfrosted raisin bread toast (1 oz) with 1 tsp tub margarine and 1 cup raw carrots
2. eight animal crackers, four pecans, and 1 cup raw peppers
3. 3 cups low-fat microwave popcorn, 10 peanuts, and 1 cup raw cucumber
4. 1 cup croutons, 1 cup salad greens, and 1 Tbsp fat-free salad dressing
5. 1/3 cup hummus for a dip (1 starch and 1 fat exchange) and 1 cup raw vegetables
6. 1/2 cup chow mein noodles (1 starch and 1 fat exchange) and 1 cup water chestnuts
7. 1/2 cup light ice cream (1 starch and 1 fat exchange) and have 1 cup raw vegetables later in the day

1800 Calorie Plan

For your midafternoon snack, you may also add 1 fruit exchange to the 1500 calorie plan's midafternoon snack. You can eat the foods together as one snack or have them separately. Some examples of one fruit serving are

1. one small apple
2. eight dried apricot halves
3. one and a half fresh figs
4. 17 small grapes
5. one medium peach
6. 1 1/4 cups fresh strawberries
7. 1 1/4 cups cubed watermelon

You also get a bedtime snack of one nonfat milk product, such as

1. 1 cup fat-free or 1% milk
2. 1 cup low-fat or fat-free soy milk
3. 2/3 cup (6 oz) of fat-free flavored yogurt sweetened with non-nutritive sweetener or about 100 calories of reduced-calorie flavored yogurt

2000 Calorie Plan

For this plan, the midafternoon snack is the same as the 1800 calorie plan above. For the night snack, you may have 1 fat-free milk, 1 starch, and 1 fat exchange. In addition to the fat-free milk choices above, examples of 1 starch exchange with 1 fat exchange are

1. three peanut butter sandwich crackers
2. 1/2 cup light ice cream
3. half of an English muffin and 1 tsp tub margarine or 1/2 Tbsp peanut butter
4. 3/4 oz pretzels and six mixed nuts
5. one reduced-fat waffle and 1 tsp margarine

Please remember to measure your snacks, just like for your meals. The key to weight control is calorie control. To make a meal plan work for a lifetime, eat within a meal plan. Make it become routine, and don't forget to exercise!

Alphabetical List of Recipes

Subject Index